PLAN A
PLAN B
PLAN C
PLAN D
PLAN E

PLAN E

How to Be Successful in Today's World

OWEN PERRY

LIONCREST
PUBLISHING

COPYRIGHT © 2023 OWEN PERRY
All rights reserved.

PLAN E
How to Be Successful in Today's World

FIRST EDITION

ISBN 978-1-5445-4058-0 *Hardcover*
      978-1-5445-4057-3 *Paperback*
      978-1-5445-4056-6 *Ebook*

For all of you who are dedicated to an active and adventurous life

CONTENTS

INTRODUCTION 9

1. RAISED IN RHODE ISLAND 17

2. ALOHA, HAWAII 37

3. MOVING TO MEXICO 59

4. BUILDING A UNIQUE PARTNERSHIP IN PUERTO VALLARTA .. 75

5. WINS AND LOSSES IN CABO SAN LUCAS 91

6. ALL MY LEARNING COMES TOGETHER IN LORETO 113

CONCLUSION 129

ACKNOWLEDGMENTS 139

ABOUT THE AUTHOR 141

INTRODUCTION

Until I was an adult, the only vacation I had ever been on was riding five hours in a station wagon to visit my grandmother in Binghamton, New York.

In the summer, when my dad got time off from his job in the Navy, my whole family piled into that car: my parents in the front, my dad driving and chain smoking the entire way, my older sisters on the bench seats in the middle rows, and the rest of us in the back with our dogs Cricket and Fifi.

Eight of us in one station wagon, ten if you count the dogs.

Those of us in the back stretched out across our bags, no seatbelts in sight. We left early in the morning, so we made ourselves comfortable and watched the scenery go by out the back window.

Finally, we pulled up to the farm. We had been on the road for hours and hours, but it was still before noon. It was a working farm, so they'd been up for hours too.

My father showed me how to milk the cows by hand, pulling the milk out in steady streams—and then he squirted me in the face with it! He took advantage of my city-slicker innocence. I never saw it coming.

I had my siblings to play with, and there were two other kids there—maybe cousins. We enjoyed being more feral for those few days, and then we all loaded back into the car for the long ride home.

We went twice, my whole childhood, and those were the only times I've ever seen my parents travel. When we were kids, they never went to dinner, to the movies, or on vacations. (Later on, after we were all grown, they would go to a chain restaurant for dinner every once in a while.)

That was our family vacation.

My life now looks pretty different: I own and operate twelve resorts in Cabo San Lucas, Puerto Vallarta, Cancun, and Loreto. The latest resort we designed and built won World's Leading Family Resort 2021 from the World Travel Awards—even beating out Disney's Aulani resort in Hawaii. My golf course has been rated one of the top three in the world, winning World Golf Awards' Best Golf Course in Mexico (2021) and Latin America (2022).

My vacations look different too. Since becoming a developer, I've traveled all around the world. I've been to the Great Wall of China and to Tokyo; I've ridden my Harley-Davidson all throughout Europe. I've been on luxury yacht cruises through Turkey, Greece, and Italy. I've been to Switzerland, Russia, Amsterdam, Sweden, and Bora Bora.

I've been fortunate enough to be able to take my kids on vacation, and they love going to Hawaii. I hope to someday go back to Bora Bora because the people and sea life are just amazing.

And I bet you're wondering how I got from there to here.

A LION OR A SHEEP?

When I was younger, I tried to compartmentalize how I grew up from my adult life. Whenever I thought about how I started out, I would lose confidence. In my mind, I could hear a voice saying, *"What the hell do you think you're doing? Who do you think you are? You have no pedigree. You didn't even go to college!"*

As I got older, however, I gained more perspective and realized that there was no before and after; it's all *me*. I gained more confidence as I kept working hard and found success.

That's what I want to share with you.

You are likely looking for direction in life. If you're anything like I was as a young adult, you don't know which way to go. You don't have anyone inspiring you yet. You're just in the river of life, aimlessly flowing through the days.

But you're passionate about finding something that you would enjoy doing, something that will give you the happiness you're looking for.

Let me ask you an important question, one that I was asked at a pivotal moment in my life: would you rather live your life one day as a lion or live a lifetime as a sheep?

I can see part of the 5 freeway from my house in Rancho Santa Fe, California. Every morning around seven, it starts to get busy. Traffic stalls and backs up for two hours or so. Then every afternoon, from three o'clock until around six, it happens again. That's what I call life as a sheep. Every day, five days a week, fifty weeks a year, every year for thirty or forty years until you retire, in a traffic jam, waiting for *this*, standing in line for *that*.

I grew up Catholic, and I believe that our Creator (whoever you may believe that creator to be) gives you all the tools you need to independently manage your own life. You have your arms, your legs, your brain. You can learn anything you want to learn. You can take care of your body anyway you want to. You just have to be clearheaded and understand that it takes effort to get out of that river of life. To go into work the hours you want to work. To have the career you want to have, that you enjoy, and that is rewarding outside of just monetary rewards.

The person who wants to do what I do and have the results I have wants to be a lion for a day. If this is you, I think you'll be interested in what I have to say.

A CLEAR PATH

This book will provide you with a clear path to finding success in today's world.

Everybody today grows up thinking that it's going to be easy. Go to school, go to college, get a degree, and your life is set up after that. But then bam! Reality hits. It's hard to find a job. Look at how many college graduates are working at Starbucks. A recent study showed that 66 percent of people with student loans wish they had never taken on that debt, that it wasn't worth it. They went through college and found that they're still not prepared for the realities of life.

> I recently saw a list of nine classes that should be mandatory learning in school:
>
> 1. Accounting
> 2. Money management
> 3. Taxes
> 4. How to build and keep good credit
> 5. Picking the right career
> 6. Nutrition
> 7. Self defense
> 8. Time management
> 9. Self confidence
>
> Those would be great classes...but they don't teach you any of that.

Every morning when I take my son to school, I pass by homeless people sitting on the sidewalk. I talk to my son and say, I doubt that when they were your age they said, "Man, I can't wait until I grow up! I'm going to live on the streets, beg for money, and do drugs for the rest of my life!" Of course they didn't.

There's a dark cloud over society these days, and I see that a lot of motivational speakers are becoming popular again. When I started working in sales, on commission, my manager told us to tape a picture of the car we wanted on our bathroom mirror. Every morning, we were supposed to tell ourselves how much we wanted that car...and that one day, we would get it. But after six months, I never came *close* to getting a car or understanding how it was supposed to work. The people who fall for that are going to go through that cycle and end up back on the highway four to six hours a day with the other sheep.

That is not the path. Instead, having a goal and a plan is the real job.

I'm going to tell you the stories of what I went through and teach you the lessons I learned. There's not going to be one magic thing I can tell you to do that will change your life, and there's no one secret to success. My story will show you that there are quite a few things you have to learn to do right in order to get out of the passive flow of that river of life. You have to have passion, want to change, and want something more—something better.

Also what may have motivated me, may be different for you, but the reality of how to get it, remains the same. I haven't met anybody yet who didn't want to be financially independent, so let me teach you how I got here.

WHY PLAN E?

Life is rarely easy. As you'll read, I had to start at the bottom and work my way to the top. There was no easy path for me to follow—no Ivy League schools to educate me, no money to help me get started, no mentor to guide me. I had to do it all.

And you learn, going through this, that there are many challenges. But if you're determined and committed, you can get through them with an attitude to win.

Sometimes plan A doesn't work out. In fact, *most* of the time plan A won't work. So what are you going to do when your plan fails and you're faced with another obstacle? Are you going to say, "Poor me, I guess I was never meant to own my own business or work for myself?" Or are you going to do what my friend and fellow Cabo San Lucas ambassador Sammy Hagar says and keep working hard until you find success?

If plan A doesn't work, move on to plan B. If that plan fails too, you just keep working your way through the alphabet. One thing all successful people have in common: they don't stop until they find the plan that works. Each failure provides new information on the path to success.

That's a theme you'll see throughout my story.

I have a lot to share with the world. I've learned a lot, trained a lot of people, and provided motivation to people who have worked with me. When I watch the people I've worked with as objectively as possible, they seem to be better off.

But I don't say this to brag. I'm not telling stories like I'm on the top of a mountain. This is a baseline, a common sense approach in today's world. It's simple and easy enough to understand, and not so unique that you can't learn it. You can do this.

Remember, I'm not well educated. I'm not a Harvard grad. I never went to business school. That doesn't mean college is not useful—if you have a plan and a goal, a degree may be very helpful in your career. But you don't *have* to go to college to learn something. In fact, the show *Shark Tank* recently said that most of the owners of the most successful companies they invested in did not go to college. Especially now, if you're motivated to learn, anything you may need is out there and easy to access. You can learn from stories, from other people, from their plans and mistakes, failures and successes.

Learn from my story and what I got right and wrong. Learn from the life experience I've gained along the way.

If you take all the lessons I've learned, add them up across all the chapters you're about to read, you'll have a comprehensive plan for success.

CHAPTER 1

RAISED IN RHODE ISLAND

When you're getting ready to leave high school and go out into the world, you have all these hopes, desires, and dreams about what's going to happen in your life. I don't think anybody graduates and thinks, "I can't wait to work at a factory for minimum wage someday!"

My first summer after high school, I had a car, an apartment, a cute Italian girlfriend and a minimum-wage factory job. Everything was new and fun at first. But then I started settling into a routine. Before too long, summer turned into autumn, and then the cold New England winter rolled around. It was gray all the time, and the routine turned into going to work every day during the week, then going to bars and playing pool on the weekends. I wondered, *Is this going to be it for me?*

I used to drive to work and think, *I hope some rich person comes and discovers me so I can have this successful life that I've always dreamed about having!*

I didn't know how they were going to find me, or what they'd be "discovering" me for, but I kept hoping that they were out there and that they'd be able to make all my dreams come true. I held out that hope every day that somebody was going to save me and bring me to a beautiful life.

Then one morning, after working at the factory for about six months, I was driving to work on another cold, rainy, miserable day in another dreary, gloomy, New England winter. A Rod Stewart song started playing on the radio. Suddenly, it hit me: nobody was coming to save me. There was no mysterious figure out there who was going to swoop in and help me figure out my career, put me through school, or give me life guidance.

In that moment, responsibility for my life was transferred from some imaginary hero to *me*. If I wanted to change things, I was going to have to help myself.

Looking back at this moment in my life, it turned out to be one of the most important events that impacted my future.

YOU'RE GOING TO HAVE TO HELP YOURSELF

From that point on, I took responsibility for 100 percent of my life and what was going to happen to me. Instead of living a fantasy life, I woke up to a cold, hard reality—and I call that a blessing. I look back and thank God that happened to me, because it put my life in my own hands.

After that, I wasn't waiting for somebody to come help me or take me away. I wasn't scared of failure; instead, it was liberating to know that my future was all on me. I came to the conclusion that anything I was going to have in life, I would have to go out there and get it for myself. Santa Claus wasn't coming, and Disney princesses are the only ones who get saved.

This has to happen for everybody at some point. Once you take control of your own life and you're not dependent on anybody, it really is empowering.

There's no one thing that's going to magically happen to change your life. Nobody is coming to help you. For things to change in your life, you have to start helping yourself.

If you're stuck in an inner city, or you don't have a good family, or you look around and feel like you don't have any options besides barely hanging onto life, and you want to get out of that situation, how are you going to do it? You can dream at night that somebody is going to come find you, save you, and take you out of that. You can get government assistance or a minimum-wage job and make just enough money to pay your rent. But how does a person on the bottom with limited options find a way to get to the top when generations of their family have never made it?

Empower yourself to find a solution. This can come in many different ways, but you have to consciously recognize at your core that you are in this life alone. We all hope that good things happen, and they do…But when you understand to the core of your being that you are in charge of your life, you are the one who is going to make it work—and that you are the one who needs to keep learning how to grow—that is the foundation of being an adult.

For me it started by reading books. The first one I read was *Think and Grow Rich*, which I'll tell you more about in Chapter

3. For now, let me just say that I recently went to a bookstore in London with my daughter and saw a new edition of this book in the bestseller section, so it is still popular today!

Instead of just dreaming of the top, you have to take the first step that puts you on the path to the top: take responsibility for your life. After all, goals are just a dream with a plan.

From there, you need to perform self-analysis to understand where you're at and what you need to be doing. If you have good friends you can trust, ask them, "Hey, tell me the truth. What do you think is going on?"

Look for someone who has the life that you want; then learn what they did to get where they are. That's the best way to start moving forward, of opening up your mind so you can formulate a plan. I gravitated toward successful people like Bill Gates and Steve Jobs, younger guys who went on to make it big. I mean, Steve Jobs created Apple out of his garage! Why couldn't I do something similar? That's when I first started to ask, *Why not me?*

If you don't have a career, start looking around at who is already successful at what you want to be doing. Educate yourself on what they did to get there, and then work backwards until you get to the point you're starting from. Now, instead of moving forward on some murky path, you can begin to follow in their footsteps. Everybody has their own journey, but at least you'll have a starting place for your forward momentum, which is the most critical part.

Instead of focusing on the negative and asking, "Why me?" look at the positive things you want and ask, *"Why not me?"*

Once you decide to start doing something for yourself in a positive way, it creates an energy. Momentum builds, and that momentum is going to start opening doors to opportunities because you're out looking for them instead of sitting back, waiting for them to find you. You don't want to rely on luck because I find that when luck does come around, it's the result of the momentum that has been created by your efforts.

Just get started. Start looking, start applying yourself—and start *helping* yourself.

LET'S REWIND TO MY CHILDHOOD

What led to me working at that factory, for minimum wage, on that cold wintery morning? And how did I get from there to here?

If the trajectory of my life story is "from rags to riches" (or, more accurately, "from a lower blue-collar life to cruising the Med on my yacht"), then my childhood in Rhode Island would be the "blue-collar neighborhood" stage.

I grew up in Conimicut, Rhode Island, a little town near the airport, on the Providence River by Narragansett Point. My mother was a stay-at-home mom when I was younger, and my father was in the Navy, in a construction battalion called the Seabees. He was stationed away from home for ten months out of the year. I didn't know this about him at the time, because he was a very reserved man who did not talk much at all, but he served in three major wars: at the tail end of World War II, in the Korean War, and at the beginning of the Vietnam War. He was mostly away from home most of my childhood.

My parents have six kids, and I came along second to last. It wasn't easy. There were eight of us living in a three-bedroom house. We were Catholic, so my mother used to drag us to church every Sunday. She made all our clothes, cooked, cleaned the house, and took care of all of us. There was no money for house cleaners or babysitters.

Summers were fun because we were by the bay. In the wintertime, everyone went to the roller-skating rink to hang out because it was freezing outside.

I was always curious and looking for adventure. I loved to cruise around on my bike and discover anything new I could find in my neighborhood. I'd set out to go as far as I could, with no set plan, losing track of time before I made my way back.

My mom was very strict about being home in time for dinner when my father was away. One day, I came home an hour late. Everyone was in the kitchen, all my siblings and even a couple of their friends, and she pulled down my pants and spanked me right there in front of everyone. I never came home late again—and even now, I'm religiously on time for everything.

After school, I had a paper route. One bone-chillingly cold, ugly, snowy day, I told my mom, "I can't do my paper route; I'm sick." (It was a *really* horrible day!)

She said, "Well, people have to have their newspaper, so I'll do your route for you."

Then she put on her jacket and did my whole route. When she came home, she was shivering and soaked to the bone. I was so ashamed—I wasn't *actually* sick—and I never shirked a responsibility again, ever, for the rest of my life. My mom set an amazing example; she did what had to be done because someone had to do it.

By the time I was twelve years old, my father had retired from the Navy—after traveling for twenty-five years—and he moved back home to work for the water department. He wasn't very talkative, but he was a stable, economic earner. As soon as he got home from work, he just plopped down on the sofa, smoked, and watched TV. That was his life. I think they coined the term "couch potato" after him. I understand now that he comes from a different generation, but growing up, my dad never took me to a ball game, and he spent absolutely no time with us kids. We were on our own.

High school was almost a non-event in the lower, blue-collar neighborhood where I grew up. There were a lot of kids running around and not too many parents in sight. They were either at work, or they were alcoholics, or divorced.

A lot of the guys I grew up with quit school when they turned sixteen and got a job, because it was legal and their families could use the money. So most of my social life outside of school was with friends who didn't go to school any longer. In fact, I'm the only one from the neighborhood kids I grew up with who actually graduated high school.

We had to take the bus to school. One day, when I was in the 10th grade, one of my friends and I were on the bus when he started a fight with another kid. He was a troublemaker, with tattoos on his knuckles that said HELL, but the other kid turned on my friend and started beating him up, and I had to jump in to pull the guy off.

After school, my friends and I met up at the field to play baseball; it was something to do after school. The kid from the bus came over and started yelling at us, calling us names. So we went after him, all five of us against this one kid. He stopped at the edge of the field and, just as we caught up to him, he yelled, "I'm going to get you guys!" Then he pulled out a knife he'd hidden in the grass.

He saw me, the person who had pulled my friend off him on the bus, so he jumped after me. My friends were stunned, and they just stood there. He knocked me to the ground and got on top of me, trying to push the knife into my chest. I frantically wondered, *What should I do?*

I grabbed the knife with my hand on the blade and pulled it away from him. He was so shocked to see me do that, he ran away. I went home with a deep cut across my palm, all the way from the base of my thumb to my little finger.

My mom asked, "What happened to you?"

I quickly made up a story: "I was taping my baseball bat and the knife slipped when I cut the tape, and I sliced my hand."

I had to go to the emergency room and ended up with thirty stitches. While we were there, a policeman came in looking for me. It turns out the kid had gone home and told his mother what had happened, and she was afraid it would turn into a gang fight so she called the cops. I had to do an interview with the police, and we were finally able to get the matter resolved, but I still have the scar to this day.

The next day, I had to go to school with this big bandage on my hand. As I walked in, the principal stopped me at the door and said, "Hey, we don't want any problems here. If you're going to cause trouble, I want you to leave right now."

I was so tired of this mess I hadn't meant to get myself into—I was just trying to protect my buddy. I said, "No, I'm cool. Nothing's going to happen."

That was the kind of environment I grew up in.

ROCKIN' THROUGH HIGH SCHOOL

I kept going to school and around eleventh grade, some of my friends and I started a rock band.

My girlfriend's brother was the lead singer, I played rhythm guitar, and another friend was on the drums. We played mainly at our houses and some local bars, and we also played the senior year talent show at the high school. We were living the life, and we thought we were the coolest thing since rock and roll was invented.

Boston was *the* place to go for live music, the music capital of New England, where everything happened. So the three of us and our girlfriends decided to take the train from Providence all the way up to Boston, to see Aerosmith. We dressed up as rock and roll as we could and walked around the Boston Commons. Then, being rock and rollers, we decided to switch girlfriends for the night. We were sixteen or seventeen years old, but we thought we were going to be the next Aerosmith.

In the summertime, we went to so many concerts at the Providence Civic Center—Kiss, Aerosmith, and I even remember seeing Rod Stewart. At the end of the show, these silver ping-pong balls all dropped from the ceiling. It was amazing. We would also hitchhike to outdoor summer concerts and sleep on the ground.

I was not a good student. I wasn't that interested in school, and most of my friends weren't even there, having already left to join the workforce. In my senior year, my mom told me, "Son, you came this far. You must put in a little bit of extra effort and graduate so you can do what you want to do later."

I said to her, "Don't worry about it. I'm going to be really rich one day."

She replied, "Well, I think you should still finish up school."

So I finished the last half of the year and I passed. I didn't know if I was going to be rich because I'd be a rockstar or anything like that; I just had this feeling of "Oh, I'm going to be rich one day."

There's a saying, "There's a spot in music for everyone." That's true, if you make that commitment, but it might be just performing weddings or something similar. Something like 98 percent of people never make any money with their music, but I thought I was going to do it somehow.

After I graduated from high school, my mother still would not let me bring my girlfriend up to my bedroom at the house. At that age, the hormones were raging so I wanted to get my own place. I sold my guitar to get enough money for a deposit on an apartment, and my friend and I went in together on a two-bedroom place. That was the end of my music career.

WORKIN' HARD FOR THE MONEY

Once I had an apartment, I had to get a job because rent was due every month.

I didn't have a path to follow, so I had never planned for college. There wasn't the money for it anyway. There was no career I could think of that made me say, "Oh my gosh, I want to do that." I was still in a discovery-of-life phase. A lot of kids have parents who can afford to send them to college and let them figure it out there, but I didn't have that ability. I'd always had this desire to be successful in life. I wanted to *be* somebody, but I'm sure everyone thinks that when they're seventeen.

I had always worked, but mostly did things like paper routes and summer jobs. There was a baseball batting range at Rocky Point, an amusement park where people would go to hit baseballs and, every summer, I would shag those baseballs all night. I made some pocket money, but I'd never had a full-time job before.

Back then, we looked for jobs in the classified ads of the newspaper. It was so disappointing. I was the only one in my neighborhood who had graduated high school, thinking life was automatically going to go smoothly, but there weren't a lot of jobs available. Rhode Island has high taxes and only a few companies are based there; it's not an economic powerhouse.

I saw that a factory was hiring and paying minimum wage. I applied and got hired. I was lucky to get that job because the only other job available that I was qualified for was a gas station attendant.

My first day, I walked in the door of this huge factory and there was the whole assembly line, stretched out as long as a football field. That's where new people started: eight to five on the line with a half-hour lunch break in the middle, punch your timecard in, punch your timecard out.

It was elementary work; no brain power needed, just assembling parts all day every day, and then passing them on down the line. It was the same thing, over and over again, every day the same, over and over and over again. We made big, industrial, high-impact printers, the size of dishwashers. I was in the yoke-assembly department, and I just did the best I could. Before I left, I became the team leader of my area—I was very proud of that. They commended me for being dependable and intelligent enough to do the job.

And I was intelligent—not book educated, but life educated. I could look into the future at the factory and see where it was going to go. I knew that every five or ten years, I'd progress farther down the assembly line until I made it to the other end by the exit doors and, after working thirty years, I could retire. That's what happened in the lives of people who stayed working there. But I thought, *Hell no! I don't want that to be my future.*

By then, my mother was working as the night manager at Dunkin' Donuts, after many years as a stay-at-home mom. She was basically a single parent while my dad was away with the

Navy. I would wake up in the morning and there would be a box of donuts in the kitchen, and that was breakfast every day for years. I still can't touch a donut today.

But there was an auto body shop in the back of the Dunkin' Donuts building. I had first gotten the hand-me-down car that my family used, but it took so much work to keep it going. So when I got this job, my mother said, "They have this car they just fixed, and he's willing to sell it to us for a good price."

It was a white, '68 Cadillac convertible—that car was something to look at, and it was in good shape. She cosigned for a loan, and I got the car.

Then I had one more thing I had to pay for.

> That Cadillac was so big, we could fit eight of us in it. My friends and I would drive up to Newport, this island off the coast where the Rockefellers and Vanderbilts had built mega mansions, to go dancing. Somebody took one of those old mansions and turned it into a nightclub called Shamrock Cliff. They played disco music in the big ballroom of this Gilded Age mansion. We spilled out onto the balconies, across the lawn, with the Newport Bay Bridge lit up in the background. (And the state of Rhode Island had just lowered the legal drinking age from twenty-one to eighteen, so it was perfect timing for us!)
>
> It was a spectacular time—but life would take me in a bad direction before I finally found my path.

WHAT OTHER OPTIONS DID I HAVE?

After I had the realization that no one was coming to help me, I considered going to junior college. I have a very analytical mind, so I decided I wanted to be an electrical engineer. I did my research and started saving money to pay for tuition. (With both of my parents working, we weren't poor enough to get government assistance, but there was no money for college.) I could only afford to go to school part time, because I'd have to keep working to pay for it, so it would take me six to eight years to earn that degree. That seemed like too long, with no guarantee that it would ultimately pay off.

During this time, a couple of my friends who had quit high school to become construction workers or other trade workers decided to get away from the brutal New England winters. It was always the dream to move to Florida and find a job. It was sunny most of the year there. In Rhode Island, I hadn't seen a house newer than a hundred years old. Our neighborhood was already completely built out, but Florida still had new neighborhoods emerging.

I considered moving to Florida too. A friend of mine was going to drive his van down, and he said I could ride with him, to split the driving. He wasn't the type of person I thought was serious; he wasn't going to make anything good happen, so I didn't do it. He ended up coming back thirty days later anyway. Most of the other guys moved back too. Those big dreams of moving away to do something different never lasted very long. The guy who had been the "cool kid" while we were teenagers ended up becoming the school janitor.

I even considered joining the military, just to be able to get out of Rhode Island. My dad had never talked to me about his career, about my work—nothing about life. If my father had said five words to me throughout all my teenage years, that would have been a lot. I didn't have a source of inspiration or career counseling. He was a good provider, and we always had food on the table, but other than that he was just checked out. His mom had only been sixteen years old when she had him, and he had joined the military as soon as he could, just to get out of upstate New York.

I just couldn't see what other options I had. If another opportunity hadn't come up when it did, I probably would have ended up joining the military.

Around the same time, one of my older sisters came home for a visit with her fiancé and told us they were moving from Las Vegas to Hawaii. I talked to them a bunch that night, trying to understand what exactly her fiancé did—something about real estate sales.

I asked them, "Hey, do you think I could move out there too?"

My sister said, "Yes, of course! Come with us!"

But after that, her fiancé pulled me aside and said, "Listen, man, I ain't gonna take care of you. If you want to come out, I'll help you get started, but I'm not paying your rent, and I'm not paying for your food. Make sure you get a round-trip ticket in case you don't make it."

I understood what he was saying, but I really liked the idea of living in Hawaii, and I wanted to go.

I always thought if I could get out of my hometown, then I could be more successful. Rhode Island seemed small and was no place to advance. I once went to an electrical company that was hiring, and there were eighty people in line for two job openings. Nothing was going to happen for me there, that's for sure. After looking at people who had been there for generations, I knew no success stories were going to come out of my neighborhood.

I thought if I could just put myself out there, where other progressive people were, I could become part of the group I wanted to be in. I saw people who were doing good things and out exploring life, not being potheads, sitting around playing video games all day. I wanted to be around people who were working, who had energy, and who were looking for ways to start a business.

I just had to find a way to get there.

SAVING UP TO MAKE IT HAPPEN

So I went to work, did my job, and saved every penny I could.

I also got another job as a night clerk at Cumberland Farms, which was a convenience store like 7-Eleven. I worked five days a week at the factory and five nights a week at Cumberland Farms. For eight months, I worked two jobs, getting up early to work at the factory, then going straight to work at Cumberland Farms before going home to fall asleep and getting up to do it all over again the next day.

One morning, I was only half awake as I drove to work, trying to brush my hair in the rearview mirror. A car stopped suddenly in front of me, and I smashed right into it.

I pulled over to the side of the road. The other person's car was fine, but my car was not drivable. It was leaking oil and water from the front. *What am I going to do? How am I going to get to work?*

Just then, my father pulled up. He rolled down his window and asked, "You get into an accident?"

Obviously. "Yeah."

"Are you okay?"

"Yeah."

Then he rolled up the window and drove off—without even offering me a ride to work. Fortunately, a friend of mine drove by and stopped to help me.

That accident just added an unexpected expense, delaying my plans. I had to fix my car, pay off my car loan, sell the car, buy a plane ticket, and save up money to live in Hawaii. And it was all on me now. I didn't have a rich uncle or somebody I could call and ask them to give me money or make the path easier.

Additionally, it turned out that, unbeknownst to me, my girlfriend's Italian family—her mother cooked this amazing Italian food, so everything at her house smelled delicious—was part of the New England mafia. I didn't learn this until after I'd been her boyfriend for four years! Her stepfather, a councilman for Federal Hill in Providence, ended up going to jail. Her brother, a friend of mine who'd been in my high school band, was arrested for robbery.

The family was being investigated, and I stumbled onto the investigators' radar. I was pulled over frequently, getting hassled by the police more and more because they thought I was part of it all. (After all, what teenager drives a white Cadillac convertible?!) Everybody was getting into trouble, and I thought, *If I stay here, nothing good is going to happen to me.*

That added a little pressure to do something to get out of there. It felt like my world kept getting smaller and smaller.

Finally, after eight months of just working, saving, and trying to stay out of trouble, I bought a one-way plane ticket from Rhode Island to Hawaii, flying through Chicago. I had to buy my ticket months in advance to get the cheapest fare. I continued working and managed to save up another seven hundred dollars.

Once I actually had my ticket, it became *real*. I was getting out of there!

Before I left, I didn't sleep well for two weeks, and when I did, I kept having this recurring dream: I was in my forties, did not find success, and had to move back home with my parents. I was a complete failure in life! It was horrible; I had that dream for so long. Every once in a while, I still have it, waking up in my mother's house, all my successes disappearing like *they* were the dream.

Anytime you do something outside what's normal in your life, you're going to have some fears about what could go wrong. Fear is a prerequisite for success. It's natural; it happens to everybody. But fear is also an emotion, and you can overcome it.

That's one of the lessons you hear a lot from anybody who has been successful: you have to overcome these fears. You find out so much about yourself once you do.

That inner voice will be creative and come up with everything that can go wrong. Instead of giving into it, evaluate the decisions you made and make sure you have a plan. Examine the steps and see what makes sense. The fear doesn't go away, but you can use it to motivate yourself.

I had a lousy job, I wasn't going to college, and there were no opportunities for anything where I lived. I was so scared that I would come back a complete failure. If I tried to make it out there and struck out, what other options would I ever find in life? It was a thin thread, but I reminded myself that even if the worst happened, at least I'd get to see Hawaii.

That fear didn't go away. It was so scary to think about moving to Hawaii. I'd never left the state of Rhode Island except for that trip to my grandparents' farm in Binghamton, New York.

But I didn't let fear hold me back, and I got on the plane.

I was on my way.

CHAPTER 2

ALOHA, HAWAII

I was so excited to be on that plane to Hawaii. I was twenty years old and finally experiencing my first time flying anywhere. Adrenaline kicked in once I realized I was really on my way. The flight attendants all wore flowers in their hair, and Hawaiian music played over the speakers. I thought it was so fun and exotic.

When we landed, it was a beautiful tropical day in the airport—nothing like the cold October day I'd left behind in Rhode Island. I didn't realize then that it was warm there all year round. I took the Wiki-Wiki bus to meet my sister at baggage claim, where she greeted me with a lei. She took me to the apartment she and her fiancé, Steve, had in Honolulu, in Makiki, where Barack Obama grew up. In fact, he was probably there at that same time!

My sister and Steve only had a one-bedroom apartment, and they wanted to keep the living room for watching TV, so I slept on the lanai, in a sleeping bag on a lounge chair—and I still had to pay half the rent! I didn't mind, though, because my journey was finally beginning. When I woke up the next morning, I thought, *You're in Hawaii. You're actually living here!*

I walked through each day amazed at all the new things I was experiencing. I came from such a different place. In Hawaii, it was always sunny and people walked around in shorts and tank tops. No more miserable, gray, overcast, bone-chilling winters, just palm trees everywhere and beautiful sunsets. It was so exciting living in this tropical paradise, and I felt like every fiber of my being was awake and alive!

Rent was seven hundred dollars a month, and I had to pay half. With the seven hundred dollars I had in my pocket, all my savings left from working two jobs all those months, I only had enough money to make it two months—if I never spent a penny on anything else. I knew I had to get to work.

I had hardly anything with me—I barely owned anything, period—so Steve gave me some of his old clothes to wear, and I started going to work with him. Steve dressed well and drove a Porsche, so he looked like he was doing well in life.

My eyes were wide open as I tried to take it all in. I'd never been anywhere before, and now here I was in Hawaii, a melting pot full of people from all over the world. The people living there were so progressive, and it was so new and exciting to the wide-eyed, innocent, naïve kid I was back then. I'd never met people from Australia, China, and England back in Rhode Island.

I thought Steve had a real estate job, but it turned out that he worked in sales for a timeshare company. He told me I could make a thousand dollars a week doing it! I just had to get a

Hawaiian real estate license. This was the very beginning of the vacation-ownership business, which started with the overdevelopment of condominiums in Las Vegas, Florida, and the Caribbean. So many condos were built that they couldn't sell all of them, so someone came up with the marketing idea of selling those units by the week, to people on vacation.

Most of the salespeople and managers working there were from Las Vegas. Even in Hawaii, they wore high-end, dressy, three-piece suits and ties—not Aloha shirts. A lot of them were ex-lounge acts, singers, or comedians, so they had big personalities, like something out of the Frank Sinatra Rat Pack days. They were very professional and took sales very seriously. If you lied in your presentation, you were out, immediately. They didn't tolerate that; this was a serious career with a strict environment. I thought it was amazing to get to work with them at such a young age.

Steve and I did what was called hospitality sales. The way it worked was we had to get people to come in and take a tour, and then the more experienced salespeople would sell to them. At night, we would go out and walk around Waikiki, trying to invite people to see the presentation. We got twenty dollars if a client showed up for the free breakfast the next morning and stayed for the presentation.

In the morning, I would greet the people who showed up and have breakfast with them. Then, I'd give them tours of the models and tell them how the timeshares worked. People were very open-minded about vacation rentals at that time. They would walk in for a free breakfast and a couple of Don Ho show tickets and walk out hours later with a five-thousand-dollar purchase!

I had never sold anything before in my life, but I got a couple of sales my first month and I made a couple hundred dollars, which seemed like good money at the time. I thought it was going to be so easy. I mean, seriously, who *doesn't* want to own a condo in Hawaii?

OBSTACLES TO OVERCOME

I met so many new people and learned a lot about different cultures. Living in Hawaii changed me in so many beautiful ways—exactly as I'd hoped it would when I worked and saved to start this adventure.

But although Hawaii is very tropical, living there wasn't always paradise. There were still obstacles I had to learn to overcome, just as there are on any big undertaking. With my positive attitude and willingness to learn, though, I felt like I was ready for anything!

After working to get people to come to timeshare presentations for a little while, I realized that there was somebody else on the streets doing the exact same thing every ten feet. Tons of people flew to Hawaii on vacation and decided to stay there, and we were all competing for the same commissions. It was like the Wild West.

After I'd been working there for about three months, I started to get the feel of the job. I was doing okay, made a couple of sales, and was beginning to get a positive vibe out of this huge decision I'd made. Then I walked into work and the company manager pulled me aside. He said, "I'm sorry, you can't work here anymore. We don't allow relatives of managers to work here."

It turned out that Steve, who was the assistant manager and who took care of his parents, had gotten his mother a job in the same sales room. Well, the company found out that he had both his mother and his fiancé's brother working there, and they were adamant that they didn't want family working there—so I was fired.

I stood there in shock and thought, *Holy shit! What are my options now?*

I didn't want to go back home as a failure. Besides, there was nothing back there for me. I'd just be in a deeper hole than when I left. But I didn't have a plan B, and I only had a couple hundred bucks in the bank.

I started walking down Kalakaua Avenue, the main street in Waikiki, when I ran into my sister. I told her what had happened, and she could see how shell-shocked I was.

She told me, "I'm sorry that happened, but it's not your fault. I know people at this new company that's hiring. Let me see if I can get you in."

She was the executive secretary for a guy who had worked for the owners of American Vacation Club back in Las Vegas. With her help, I got a job at a startup called Discovery Bay, still doing timeshare presentations, but for a much smaller company with a really nice condominium project, right across from the Ilikai hotel where *Hawaii 5-0* was filmed. There were only six or seven of us working there, so we had to go out and get our own clients, and we earned commission on the ones we brought in.

I met some guys my age and with similar goals—we wanted to

get rich—including Dan Riordan, a really good-looking dude who had played on the Washington Huskies football team. He was tall and muscular with blond hair and blue eyes. People would just stop on the street and start talking to him, so I would wait for that to happen and then try to talk those people into coming to the breakfast and tour. (Dan now has six kids and owns one of the biggest pawn shops in Maui!)

I met a lot of Australians because Australia had a deal that if you worked there for twenty years, you got six months off with pay. The Australians on vacation in Hawaii loved to stop and talk. At first, I had a more reserved, closed-off personality, so I had to really fight that to open up and talk to people. But if you can't do that, you can't sell, especially on commission.

The upside of working on commission is you have the potential to make a lot of money. The downside is that you could work all week and end up not getting a paycheck at all. That happened to me a lot in the first year I was in Hawaii. I would make some sales and earn commissions, but it wasn't consistent money—and, worse, it wasn't something I controlled. When I worked forty hours a week at the factory job, I knew exactly how much I was making and when I would get paid. Some weeks in my sales position, I didn't get a sale at all.

It was scary not knowing how much money I'd make each week, but it was a very fun time in my life. It was a great place to be in your early twenties. And I found ways to survive, even when I didn't have much money. When I got paid, there was this great buffet at a nearby hotel. They had roast beef and other amazing stuff to eat, all for under ten dollars. If I had the money, I would go there and eat all I could.

The International Marketplace also had a Mongolian barbecue place that served a big platter of noodles with a sprinkling of pork and veggies. For five bucks, that was a substantial meal.

Another time, I heard about a promotion at McDonald's. Hawaii was having a penny shortage at the time, and the McDonald's in Waikiki announced that if you brought in five dollars of pennies, they would give you a five-dollar bill—and a free hamburger.

I went to my piggy bank, counted out five hundred pennies, and walked to McDonald's. (Every kid has a piggy bank and, yes, I brought mine to Hawaii with me.)

Waikiki had such a cool vibe, and it was buzzing that night. Michael Jackson was popular then, and as I walked, I saw a group of local Hawaiian kids—maybe thirteen or fourteen years old—dancing to a big boombox blasting "Billie Jean." When I got to the McDonald's, I saw that it was packed. It was around seven o'clock, dinnertime for most people, and there were eight or ten lines, each with about twenty people in them, with more coming in all the time. It was *busy*.

I finally got up to the register, all those pennies held in my cupped hands. I didn't have them in rolls or anything, so I set them in a pile on the counter and the cashier began counting them. They counted so slowly, "two, four, six…," organizing them into small piles of ten cents each. Everybody in line behind me was staring at me, and I was sweating.

Finally, they had fifty piles with ten pennies in each. They gave me my five-dollar bill and a hamburger—the trip was a success! I enjoyed that hamburger very much, and I left smiling, satisfied with how creative I'd been to get my dinner.

LIVING THE *OHANA* LIFESTYLE

When I started working at Discovery Bay, I decided to move out of my sister's apartment. I didn't have a lot of options of where to live—I couldn't afford an apartment on my own—but I met this guy named Don at work. He was in sales too, and he had a one-bedroom apartment right inside Waikiki by the Ala Moana shopping center. I rented his couch for a few months.

In my first year in Hawaii, I worked ten- to twelve-hour days, seven days a week. I didn't really take any days off. I just spent the time getting to know the island, learning what I was doing, and discovering the rhythm of living and working in Hawaii. I was a worker, always the first person to arrive in the morning, and the last one to leave. I was there to learn how to do a job and to eventually have a career I could make good money from.

After I had been there for about twelve months, learning how to make a living on commission pay, Royal Aloha Vacations asked me to come work with them. They were a growing, successful company; the condos they were selling were at the Aloha Towers, and the new sales room was at the Seaside lanai. That was where this boy became a man.

Unfortunately, the company wasn't very well organized, and it wasn't doing great. About three or four months after I started working there, I showed up for our daily meeting, at eight o'clock, but nobody from management showed up. Twenty of us just sat there in the sales room, wondering what to do next. There were no tours, nothing—and they never told us anything. Overnight, my sister, her fiancé, and the general manager just took off for a new job in Lake Tahoe. I didn't want to follow them—moving every few months was not my idea of stability.

That's when I learned never to depend on somebody else for my work. I wasn't going to do anybody any favors anymore. *I was going to be in control.* I was going to make the right business decisions based on what I wanted to accomplish.

I went back to Discovery Bay and worked there for a while. Then I went back to the American Vacation Club because they were the best in Waikiki at the time.

In my second year in Hawaii, I started taking one morning off a week to go to the beach. Sundays are a big day in tourism, check-in day, so I would usually have either Friday or Saturday mornings off to explore or hang out on the beach with some of the guys I worked with.

We worked near the Sheraton, by the Royal Hawaiian and the original hotels of Waikiki. At the end of the row of resorts, there were stairs going down to Waikiki Beach and that's where we'd all hang out, people watching or oiling ourselves up and letting the sun bake us. These local Hawaiian guys also hung out there. They would go to the ABC Stores, buy straw mats for two dollars, and rent them to the tourists for five bucks. They cracked me up with their ingenuity and entrepreneurial spirit.

I no longer felt like the same person, fresh from Rhode Island. I felt like I was part of Hawaii.

I started meeting different people and making new friends from all over. One guy, Ricky DeMartino, came from Las Vegas, where his family had a very successful Italian restaurant called DeMartino's. (Frank Sinatra even ate there!) Ricky came out to Hawaii to get into sales, so we became friends as we worked together.

He had a Stingray T-Top that he shipped to Waikiki. I never owned a car the whole time I was in Hawaii, because I could never afford it, but once Ricky and I became friends, I would give him gas money and we would cruise all around the island. We went to beach parties and luaus, the Hawaiian barbecue where pits were dug in the sand and a pig was wrapped in leaves, buried with coals, and roasted for hours.

One of my best days ever in Hawaii was when we went to a luau in Makaha, way on the west side of the island. It was a beautiful day, and we cruised down the highway in Ricky's car with the top down and the radio blasting Bob Seger. The scenery was so picturesque, it felt like it was out of a movie.

That year, maybe inspired by Elvis's "Blue Hawaii," everybody wanted to be a surfer dude. I surfed a little bit in Waikiki on a longboard, but nothing like the locals who rode the big waves. My friends and I didn't have a lot of money, but we were determined to explore Hawaii. Three or four of us would chip in to rent a car, and we'd drive to all the beaches—North Shore, Banzai, and Sunset—to see the real surfers braving the thirty- and forty-foot waves. It was so beautiful, just an amazing experience, and we had a lot of fun.

On one of these trips, we got up early on a Saturday morning and drove the hour and a half to North Shore. On the way, when we were close to Sunset Beach, one guy said, "Hey, stop here."

There were a lot of cattle ranches on the North Shore, and we stopped right by one. Our friend got out of the car, jumped over the fence, ran into the cow pasture, and came back ten minutes later with a handful of mushrooms. We went to Sunset Beach, and he passed out the mushrooms to everybody. I hadn't had breakfast, and I was pretty innocent (I'd smoked a little pot in those days but nothing else), so I thought it was just something to eat, for nutrition. I was sitting on the beach when all of a sudden it kicked in—they were magic mushrooms!

The beach was beautiful, but as I was sitting there, everything became psychedelic. The surfers moving through the water looked distorted. I wasn't sure what was going on. One surfer came out of the water all cut up and dripping blood. He had gotten smashed onto some coral by a big wave, and it took out a chunk of his skin. It was so gory, and so uniquely traumatic from my drugged perspective, that I never surfed again after that.

Waikiki was also a great place to go to the nightclubs. One time, a guy we worked with invited us to go sailing the next day on his new boat. Even though we knew we had to get up at six, we stayed out drinking until four in the morning. The next morning, the water was incredibly rough, with eight- to ten-foot swells. I've never been so sick in my life.

It was an adventure to be young there, but it was an expensive one!

LEARNING A LESSON

By my third year in Hawaii, I was living in a nice studio apartment at the Marine Surf. The building had an Italian restaurant, Mateo's, on the first floor and then condos that were individually owned and some people rented to tenants. My rent was three hundred and fifty dollars a month.

I was twenty-three, and I liked to go out, often spending more money than I should at the nightclubs. Then, one month, I couldn't make rent. I paid the landlord what I had—about two hundred dollars—and promised I'd get the rest to him as soon as possible.

I fully intended to do just that…but the nightclubs were calling, and again I spent too much. I scraped together another fifty dollars and told the landlord again that the rest of his money was coming, but then I didn't get a commission that week.

One day, after being about three weeks behind on the rent, I came home and saw a note under the door. It was a Hawaiian-style threat:

"You're hereby notified to vacate Marine Surf apartment 608 within five days upon receipt of this notice, or pay $150. Failure to comply will result in assistance from the sheriff's office. Or I may request a husky Samoan to assist me in duties as an owner/landlord."

I immediately figured out how to pay what I owed, but I had to borrow fifty dollars from a friend—and had to pay back a hundred fifty dollars!

After that, I moved out and found a roommate (a girl I was working with), and that's the only time I ever got into serious financial problems. I woke up to the seriousness of the situation and added another layer of understanding to my financial education: you have to pay your bills to survive. I'd never been threatened to be kicked out of a place to live before. It was a new experience, and for someone who thought he was guaranteed success in his life, that felt like an epic failure. How was I going to be extremely successful if I couldn't pay $150 for rent?

It wasn't easy to live in Hawaii—especially Waikiki, which is very expensive.

I called my parents to tell them what happened, because I'd never had to borrow money before. My dad answered the phone, and I told him, "I'm starting to have some problems here. I don't know what I'm going to do. I'm running out of money, and I don't know if this is the right career."

"Well," he said, "let me pass you to your mother."

When she got on the phone, she told me, "Whatever you do, we'll support you. If you want a plane ticket to come back home, I'll loan you the money. But I'm sure that if you stay, you're going to do well."

"Thanks," I said. "I'll figure it out."

I looked at other jobs, trying to think of what else I could do to earn money. I considered becoming a bellman or a waiter, but those jobs didn't appeal to me. They didn't lead to doing anything better.

Then, shortly after that call, I was walking through this park near Diamond Head and I saw a homeless guy leaning up against a palm tree with his legs out in front of him, arms crossed against his chest, and a smile on his face. I thought to myself, *If that's the worst that can happen to me—having to sleep in a park near a beach in Hawaii—I'm okay with that. I can do this.*

Of course there were a few bumps in the road, but every path in life has those bumps. What was important to me was that I didn't take the easy way out, moving back home with my parents. I knew I could make some good money where I was; I just wondered when that was going to start. I'd come to Hawaii to be rich and successful, not to subsist on tuna and crackers for dinner.

One week, I went to get my paycheck. They paid us in cash, so we would walk into the office and they'd count out our commissions in twenty-dollar bills. It didn't take long to count mine; I'd only made eighty dollars that week. As I was leaving, the next person came in, a guy named Neil Lipsky, and I paused as they kept counting: "Twenty, forty, sixty, eighty…," all the way up to two thousand dollars.

Man, I wanted to be him! *This* is what I moved to Hawaii to find! He was two years younger than me, good looking, and he was making great money. He even had a cute Hawaiian girlfriend. As I watched them drive off in his red Porsche convertible, I thought, *Oh my gosh, I'm doing this all wrong*.

I wanted to make money. I wanted to *go somewhere*, be successful, and not just survive. I could see the opportunity was there, but I had no plan to actually make it happen.

YOU NEED A PLAN

The people I worked with were all cool guys from different parts of the country and from all over the world. I was around progressive people, and we were out hustling, which was exactly where I wanted to be. We all had the same goal no matter where we were from: we wanted to make money and improve ourselves. Let me tell you, there were a lot more opportunities to be successful in Waikiki than there had been in Rhode Island!

> One day at work, the new guy on our marketing team pulled me aside and said he wasn't able to get anyone to come to see the resort...but he *was* able to lift three credit cards from tourists, and we could use them to buy whatever we wanted! I didn't even have to think about it before I said, "Listen, we are going to learn how to use our talents to make money the *legal* way."
>
> I never saw him again after that, and I knew that his plan was not the same as mine!

My two big goals were to make a thousand dollars a week and to buy some type of convertible sports car. I taped a picture of a car on my bathroom mirror and looked at it every day, like the manager of one of my first sales training classes had told us to do. I just had to say affirmations and think about what I wanted and it would show up, right? I kept saying, "It's going to happen eventually."

I thought I was doing everything right, and I fully believed that I'd wake up one morning and that car would be outside. I was young—who was I to argue that it wasn't going to happen? Maybe that's the way the world works. (Let me tell you now: the car never showed up.)

Eventually, I started to get disillusioned. I didn't know what I was going to do. I wasn't making enough money, and I was never going to get that car. It just wasn't happening. Then I committed to actually *learning* the job of sales and marketing.

Nobody ever teaches you how to take care of yourself financially, so I started looking for my own answers.

I was reading *Success* magazine when an advertisement in the back caught my eye: a book called *Get Rich In Spite of Yourself*, which they were selling for five dollars. I sent away my money, and in return I got a Xerox copy of the pages of the book in the mail.

> *Get Rich In Spite of Yourself*, by Louis M. Grafe, is a book I can highly recommend. It was first printed in 1945, and it tells the author's story of how he made money, lost it in the Great Depression, and then made his money back again.

One quote, in particular, stood out. "Provide a service to your community and you will be rewarded for it."

That clicked for me. If I could learn how to provide a service, somebody would pay me to do it. That made a lot more sense to me than putting a picture of a car on my mirror.

Then I looked at it another way: money is a payment for providing a service. Sounds simple, right? But it's so enlightening once you learn what money *really* is. Money is not something you wish for or dream about. It won't miraculously show up in your life. I couldn't just have an emotion of wanting to make a thousand dollars a week with no real plan as to how I would actually do so.

You have to have a plan, and you have to educate yourself about providing a service to this community we live in. When you provide that service, someone will pay you for it. Find the service you can provide to people, and the more people you provide it to, the more money you'll make. Boom, it's that simple.

In Hawaii, I learned how to become financially independent. Where in Rhode Island, I'd had the realization that nobody was going to come take care of me, here I learned that I could take care of myself economically. I had complete, 100 percent control over my life. If I wanted money, I knew how to make it.

When I analyzed myself, I realized that I had not been learning how to do the job better, or really even trying. I was just showing up to work every day and going through the motions, hoping to get a sale, but I wasn't in control of anything.

I would have to get an education and learn how to sell.

Living in Waikiki—that was my college, the education I needed to be successful in life. (And it wasn't a bad place to learn, with girls in bikinis on the beach!) Working on commissions was a horrible way to start that education because there was no salary, but because of that I had to learn fast: you either quit or you adapt. It takes an inner strength to make money on commission—there's no limit to how much you can make once you know what you're doing.

Working on commissions is great for an experienced salesperson, but *getting* the experience is a challenge. I learned to focus more of my time when I was at work, to get results, instead of just going through the motions and having fun. I built up my inner toughness, and that focused me too.

You have to go to work with a purpose. You need a goal. You need to know exactly what to do to reach that goal, and you have to be serious about it. Not "well, if it happens, it happens." No! You're going to find a way to *make* it happen.

That's the evolution you get when working on commissions. I'm glad I got that education because I don't know where else you can learn those lessons. They don't teach that in college.

Additionally, I learned there's no *one* thing to do to be successful and make money. It's a series of events. Even if you get a great education from a traditional college, you still have to find the right opportunity that's going to maximize that investment in your education. You have to learn how to provide a service to society. Success is not going to be automatic.

You have the ability to have whatever you want in your life. Look at me: you know where I came from, and I now have a ten-seat, 2020 Embraer Legacy 500 jet; I'm building a 160-foot yacht, and I own five houses and penthouse apartments.

So what do *you* want? What would you like to have tomorrow? When you are completely in control of how you make your money, then you have the ability to make it happen.

THINGS LOOK UP

I didn't have all that yet in my twenties, but I did know that I wanted to make a lot of money, as does any kid who grows up with very few things. My eyes had been opened even more. I just needed to get a plan and then *work*. In Hawaii, I could see all the advantages of being successful in a business life.

And that's what I did.

The first step I took was to get a complete education in how to earn money without going to college. Before, when I'd been learning sales, I'd go to trainings and sort of listen to people, but I wasn't really paying attention because I thought, *Money's money. All you have to do to earn money is show up.*

After my realization, I started buying sales books, learning everything I could, and really applying myself. I sat down with the top guys at work and asked them to talk to me about how they got to where they were. I really took control of my own education, putting significant effort into learning what I was doing so I could make good money doing it. I was a sponge.

Once I understood that main concept—that I needed to not just provide any service but provide a service where I could help people *and* make a lot of money at the same time—I never had to worry about money again.

Working on commission is an opportunity to make a lot of money—if you educate yourself to be really good at the service you're providing that pays that commission. I'd finally unlocked the secret. (And ever since leaving that factory gig back in Rhode Island, I've never again worked on salary or hourly pay; I've only been on commission, overrides, and/or profit sharing.)

Once I had that key, I consistently did better and better. I started making some good money—not enough yet to own a car or a nice place, but it was a big change. I was improving myself, and I felt like I had some structure in my life, creating a platform from which I could build a great career.

I looked around and saw that the vacation home business was growing and had started to become mainstream. I also saw that the people who really had control of their lives and careers were not the salespeople who relied on the company to give them leads that provided the whole source of their income. No, the people who controlled the business were on the *marketing* side. I decided to make the switch into marketing, creating programs to bring in clients.

To start, I worked part time at night as the assistant manager for a company owned by Debbie and Joe, a married couple out of New York, while still working my sales job during the day.

One Saturday, I had nothing going on so I went in to do some extra shifts in marketing. I saw Debbie and Joe in the office, moving furniture so they could paint the walls. They were doing everything themselves because the manager hadn't shown up for work that day to help them out. I said, "I'm not doing anything. Do you want some help?"

We painted all day, and they took me out to dinner that night. On Monday, they announced that I would be the new manager. They hadn't talked to me about it, but they liked that I had shown up to help when the old manager hadn't. So I quit my day job and became the marketing manager for them. I got paid based on how many people my team brought in, with a bonus for clients who bought. It wasn't a lot of money—five hundred to eight hundred dollars a week—but I was comfortable.

Once I became a manager, I needed to provide a service to the people on my team, so I started reading books on management. I knew that if you learn how to provide a service to one person you'll get paid, but if you learn how to provide a service to many people you could make even more money. I have always done my best to passionately educate anybody on my team, and I've always had great success.

People often have talent in some areas but lack education in others. Debbie was very creative and great at sales, but she wouldn't let us take any notes during her meetings. She felt that if we took notes we'd be able to learn what she knew, and then we'd try to take over. She was very insecure about sharing her knowledge—as many people are, because they're afraid they're going to lose their job.

When I became manager, I made it *mandatory* to take notes. I would also make copies of my instruction manuals to give to everybody. Some people looked at me like I was an idiot, but overall people were very positive.

I worked for Debbie and Joe for about a year, and during that time they made some terrible business decisions. One client didn't pay them, so they took the money out of their own pockets to pay the staff. They thought they were heroic, paying everybody even though they weren't getting paid, but they ended up going bankrupt and the company shut down.

From them, I learned to be smart, not to be a saving angel. I saw that it wasn't worth it. They tried to do everything they could to protect their people—even though they didn't have to. They already drove Mercedes, had a nice condo in a beautiful building, and lived a great life—but the people they paid still left and found new jobs. No one even thanked them or shook their hands for paying them all that time. It was a big learning experience: help people as much as you can, but not to the point where you lose your business because of it.

After that business closed, I became the night manager at the Imperial Hawaiian Resort, doing marketing for a bigger company that was better organized and better funded. It was the best company in the business, anywhere in the world, and I enjoyed working there.

During that time, I made the decision to work hard and put in the hours, to have a career first, and *then* consider getting married or having kids. I saw a couple of my friends get married and have kids, but that seemed like an anchor. Suddenly those guys couldn't take any chances in life.

I didn't have much of a social life because I was putting in ten-hour days, five or six days a week. That was my purpose, and I put a lot of effort into it. I was just starting to learn a new career, to wake up in life. Absolutely no way did I want to get married and have kids. I needed to get more established first.

By the time I left Hawaii, I still didn't own that car, but I did have an education and a career to pursue. I finally knew how to make money, and I was learning how to take care of myself financially. That's certainly more than I had when I arrived!

CHAPTER 3

MOVING TO MEXICO

After five years of living in Hawaii, I was given the opportunity to take a two-week vacation in Puerto Vallarta, Mexico.

A company out of Seattle, called Vacation Internationale, had a couple of properties in Hawaii and were beginning their expansion into Mexico. They were hiring salespeople, and a few of the guys I knew from Hawaii ended up moving to Mexico to work there. A few months later, they returned to Hawaii to recruit other people, and they asked me to go with them. I was working in marketing for a good company and they desperately wanted someone in that position. The first couple of times they asked, I said no.

Things were changing in Hawaii. Smaller developers had created some problems in the timeshare business because they were underfunded and sold properties they didn't own, so the industry shifted toward larger companies. The Hilton Hawaiian Village and Disney's Aulani opened up as vacation ownership resorts, and larger, more credible companies moved into the market.

We started being able to see a future with good management jobs—with salaries and retirement plans—where before it was strictly all commission.

Then Steve, my sister's former fiancé now, who I hadn't seen in years, came back to Hawaii and told me, "Owen, I've been in Mexico and they need someone like you down there. They don't have anybody with your expertise or your knowledge. You'd be great!"

"I don't know," I told him. "I don't speak Spanish. Hell, I don't even know where Puerto Vallarta is!"

"Just come check it out!"

The company offered me a round-trip plane ticket and an all-expense-paid stay at one of their properties. They told me to just enjoy the trip as a free vacation and we could talk after I came back. I hadn't been off the island in years (and island fever is real!), so I agreed to take two weeks off and see what the resorts in Mexico were like.

"Why not?" I said. "It's free!"

One of the guys who had moved down there was an amazing salesperson named Les Prickett. He came back to Hawaii for a little break before I left for my vacation, and we met up at a bar. Over our drinks, I asked him, "What do you think about me moving to Mexico?"

"No, Owen," he replied. "Don't do it. You're an American guy. You're going to get some girl pregnant down there, and her father is going to come after you with a shotgun and make you marry her!"

My eyes got wide, and I was nervous about going down there. Later, though, my friends told me, "Hey, don't listen to him. He's just trying to stop anybody from moving in on his territory because there's hardly anybody else in this market, so he's killing it. His sales numbers are *amazing*!"

While I wasn't sure about taking the job or moving to Mexico, especially after talking with Les, I was excited to visit my friends and see a new country. I told myself that I'd be cautious and everything would be fine.

When I got there, I saw that the resort was very nice, offering a more personal experience than I had seen in Hawaii. Hawaii was tourism on steroids—Waikiki Beach had seven thousand hotel rooms in three-quarters of a square mile, and this was just the beginning of the tourism boom in Puerto Vallarta. It was tropical, just like Hawaii, but I could feel the opportunity in the air here. We went out to dinner and then to a nightclub called Capriccio's. This place was off the charts, and everybody ended up there, dancing until four or five in the morning.

After a couple of days, I was in the office looking at the business side of the resort. They didn't give me the hard sell. They were going to find a marketing guy; if it wasn't me, they could just hire someone else.

I saw this opportunity so clearly: I would have no competition in this town, so I could make a killing, and if I didn't take this job, somebody else would. I accepted the job offer my first week there, while still on vacation, and I never went back to Hawaii. I had a couple of guys at work pack my belongings and bring it down to Mexico, and they came to work with me too.

I just knew I was going to do really well here.

AN EVER-EVOLVING PLAN

Hawaii had a very high cost of living with incredibly high taxes. A few of the guys I knew who stayed there got into good management positions, but none of them went on to have the success I had. (If I had stayed there, I probably would have ended up higher in management, but I likely wouldn't have become a resort owner. Mexico opened up a lot of opportunities to be in an ownership position.)

All you can do is put yourself in a position to grow and be successful. If you don't put yourself in that position, how is it ever going to happen? There was no guarantee of success in any of these moves I made, but I was open to the opportunity and put myself in place to achieve my goals.

You have the ability to be 100 percent in control of the life you have and what you experience. Do you want to do that work? Because it does take work. But if you put in the time and effort, you can learn so much about yourself. It's amazing. Never stop learning about yourself.

Do a self-diagnostic and meet with somebody who can help you understand where you are and what you've done. Become more aware of what changes you have to make and where you need to go to get where you want to be.

Consider the answers to these questions:

- Are you achieving your goals in life?
- Are you doing what you are passionate about?

If not, make a change before time goes by too fast and you're stuck. It's easy to just let things keep going the way they have been. You get comfortable doing something that seems good, and then bang—ten years have gone by.

A lot of people start like that...and then they get stuck. Time goes by so fast, and then they realize they're still in that job they'd promised to leave. When you hit a fork in the road, a place where you have to decide to go one way or the other, think through those decisions carefully rather than making them on autopilot.

When I performed this self-diagnostic, I knew there was absolutely no reason why I wouldn't find success and live in the penthouse someday. (After all, *why not me?*) Once I decided to become financially independent and take care of myself, I owned my life, but I still had to find the right opportunities and make the decisions that would continue leading me down that path.

In Chapter 2, I told you that you need a plan—and you do. A goal without a plan is just a dream, so you need a plan of action to achieve your goals. And, with that, you have to understand that Plan A is not going to work all the time. In fact, Plan A is almost *never* going to work.

When that happens, you can't just think, "Plan A didn't work, so it's never going to happen for me," and talk yourself out of your goal because it wasn't easy on the very first try. Changing your life takes a lot of effort and commitment. You have to have a plan, but you also have to understand that you'll need to adjust your plan—potentially many times—as you go through it.

The first plan you come up with is not likely to go the way you initially anticipated. We all want Plan A to work, and if it does, great. Put all your effort into Plan A, but if it *doesn't* work, don't throw it out the window. Take Plan A and see what worked, what helped, and then make a variation on that plan to help you aim better for your target—that's your Plan B. If Plan B gets you one step closer, then you continue fine tuning it: Plan C. Then you take Plan C and align it even more with your goal, and that's Plan D. These are not completely different plans; they are adjustments that help each plan fit better and get closer to where you want to be.

My life I usually found success with Plan E....

The sooner you take control of your life—and understand that if you're not happy and not doing what you want to do, you're the one who has to take that first step forward toward making a change—the more time you have to adjust and fine tune. Once you take that first step, the second step is a little easier than the first. The third step will be even easier, and then you're moving in the right direction.

> I love the book *Think and Grow Rich* by Napoleon Hill because it shows that many successful people failed before they found success. For example, Edison failed ten thousand times before inventing the light bulb.
>
> The book shares another story about a family of gold miners in Colorado during the Gold Rush era. They had a gold mine that had been producing for thirty years, when it suddenly stopped. They continued digging in every direction possible to try to find the gold vein again. When they couldn't, they sold the mine for pennies. The person who bought it hired a geologist who studied the mine and discovered the vein three feet away from where the original family had stopped digging. That's where I learned not to stop three feet from my goal!
>
> *Think and Grow Rich* was the first influence on me to be positive. If you don't strike gold the first time, keep trying.
>
> The title is also a good strategy: think first about the plan and what you're going to do. Then you have to *keep* thinking, because there's no automatic path to happiness and wealth. But if you do all of that, you really can grow rich!

BIENVENIDO A MEXICO

Once I'd decided to stay in Puerto Vallarta, I looked around and saw a completely virgin territory for my education.

After living in Hawaii, a melting pot with cultures from all over the world, I was no longer the naive kid from Rhode Island. When I went to Mexico, it wasn't a shock to be immersed in a new culture. Instead, I was interested in learning about the lifestyle in another country. I was open to discovering more about the world.

Everything was different in Mexico—the food, the culture, the language, the people.

Puerto Vallarta is an older fishing port, a small town with a magical feel to it. It had cobblestone streets, bars all over the place, and a unique personality full of charm. Instead of having one area where tourists stay and another where locals live, Puerto Vallarta had everyone in the same place, socializing together in the same bars and restaurants.

The company rented me this house right in the middle of town, where they filmed *The Night of the Iguana*, with Elizabeth Taylor and Richard Burton. Both of them were married to other people at the time, but that's where they started their romance. They bought houses across the street from each other and built a bridge connecting them—and I went on to live on that same street.

A few of my friends were already there, so I had a nuclear group who took me under their wing and told me what I should and should not do. Everyone I met in Mexico was so friendly to me, good human beings with the same goals I had: having a nice life and making some money.

I became good friends with Antonio Canales, the manager of the Hotel Oceano, right in the middle of the town of Puerto Vallarta. He took me driving for hours, up into the mountains of Jalisco, to the cock fights, through all the small towns and little farming communities that oozed personality, each with their own fiesta days. They'd have shows, and sometimes Vicente Fernandez would show up and sing with his touring band. There were cockfights and games of *pares y nunes* (which means "evens and odds," and it's a betting game a little like Bingo). I was the only American around, and I was invited into everyone's homes with open arms.

I had been very concerned about not speaking Spanish, especially as I was the manager. A couple of Mexican people on my team pulled me aside one day and told me, "Señor Owen, it's not important for you to speak Spanish. It's more important for us to practice our English, because with better English we can make more money."

That took the stress away. I eventually learned Spanish, but initially not knowing the language wasn't a detriment to living and working there. (Even today, in Loreto, if I speak Spanish someone will say, "Señor Owen, can you speak in English so we can practice?")

I often took Friday mornings off and went waterskiing on Bandera Bay. Then I would lay out on the beach and have a cold beer and a fresh seafood cocktail. It was so beautiful.

I also started playing golf in Puerto Vallarta, at Flamingo's golf course, which was way out of town, part of a tourism project created by the Mexican government. The course was pretty crude, and in the summertime the mosquitoes were as big as birds because of the hot, humid weather, so I learned to play fast.

Vacation Internationale had resorts in Puerto Vallarta, Mazatlan, and Acapulco, so I traveled and learned more about Mexico.

I was based in Puerto Vallarta, so that's where I began building the company and learning about Mexico's labor laws. Then the company sent me to Acapulco, which had a completely different energy—very secluded, with some of the best resorts in the world.

Acapulco's heyday was in the sixties and seventies, when all the Hollywood movie stars used to go there. I visited toward the tail end of their popularity, but the nightclubs were still vibrant.

Acapulco was like that: very alive, a little on the weird side, but an incredibly fun place.

From there, I traveled to Mazatlan. At that time, in the late 1980s and early '90s, the main businesses in Mazatlan were shrimping and tourism. There were some nice resorts, a lot of American expats living there, and it was a popular destination for college kids on spring break.

It was also the heyday of the narco culture from the cartels, but I never saw any evidence of that anywhere I've lived or visited in Mexico. There were no gun fights on the streets, and it was a shock to me when I saw movies and television shows portraying it that way. I've been in Mexico for thirty-five years and I've never seen any violence, not even a fistfight or a tourist robbed.

I liked visiting Acapulco and Mazatlan, but neither of them captured my emotions in the same way Puerto Vallarta did. I was happy living in Puerto Vallarta, which had a similar vibe as Hawaii: palm trees, coconuts, the beautiful beach, and even the same weather because they're on the same latitude. I felt so comfortable there, and that's where I met some of my best friends to this day.

FIND YOUR MOTIVATION

The work was the same as what I was doing in Hawaii, but with far less competition. In Hawaii, there were tons of big companies and we were all fighting every day for each client we could get. But in Puerto Vallarta, there was absolutely no one else doing what we did, with more tourists starting to visit, and a nice product to offer—it was easy.

Once I accepted the job, I worked seven days a week, ten hours a day most days, for three years straight. Other companies started to come into town, and I wanted to lock up all the spots and get good commitments. By the time those other companies arrived, I was already dominant in every phase. I took that time when things were good and nothing was happening, and consolidated everything I did so that nobody could come in later and take it away from me.

At that time in my life, I was twenty-five years old, and I was serious about making money. That was my number-one goal. I didn't want to be stuck in a nowhere job with a wife and kids to support, with no options about what to do next. Everything I learned in life, I watched from other people ahead of me, and I saw that most of the guys I met in their late twenties or early thirties who had kids, they instantly had to do that job. They didn't have any other choice; they had kids to support. I didn't want that; I wanted to have a career and money.

I put that pressure on myself when I was younger, because I wanted to work hard *now* and reap the rewards later. I saw a lot of my friends at that age wanting to do it the easy way now—going to the beach, chasing girls, and having parties—but that meant they would have to learn financial independence the hard way later. Most men mature in their forties, and by then they're working, married, and have kids—and *then* they have to start getting serious about making money. I wanted to get serious when I was younger, and although I didn't know it at the time, I see now how unique that motivation is.

You have to learn how to motivate yourself. Find what motivates you. This is first and foremost an internal process. What do you want, and *why* do you want that? Now look deeper. What is the purpose, the meaning behind what you want? How can you use that to push yourself?

The key to growth is to learn to use your motivation to pressure yourself in a positive way. I see some people pulling their hair out, banging their head against the table, or telling themselves, "You're a loser!" But that's not positive—and that's not the way to bring out your best.

Keep challenging yourself in a positive way. Look at books, podcasts, videos, anything that goes through a couple of layers of you, pulls out who you are, and motivates you to stay in the game and keep trying.

I emphasize staying positive because attitude is number one. I don't care where you are or what you're doing; if you're unmotivated and don't want to get out of bed or off the couch…your very first job is to turn that around. Nothing is going to just come to you unless you're really lucky, but I'd rather have that power to make things happen myself—and that starts by having a positive attitude.

I think our creator gave us the ability to control our attitude. Some days it's harder than others, but your mind is a muscle like any other in your body. If you go to the gym every day, sooner or later your body will respond and get stronger. The same is true of your mind: if you work it every day, it will respond and get stronger, and you can control your attitude.

The world is so competitive right now, with so many people doing the same job. So what's going to give you that little fraction of an edge above them? Your attitude. Your energy. The better you can keep your attitude, the better your life is. Two different people can have a very similar skillset but their attitudes may be completely different—and that can elevate one above the other.

You also want your motivation to help you be positive, because that motivation will help you get through not just current tough times but future ones as well.

In Puerto Vallarta, I began the practice of not getting out of bed in the morning until I had a positive thought. I still follow this discipline today. Try it and you'll see that it affects your whole day if you wake up in bed and start your morning with a positive thought.

If you're not sure how to start, you can borrow the affirmation I say in the morning, "I'm awake, I'm alive, I feel great."

Habits can be easy to set and difficult to break, whether positive or negative. You can start by smoking a cigarette or two here and there and end up with a lifelong addiction. But you can also start by waking up with a positive thought every day, and that can become a lifelong addiction too.

Anything good in your life—your career, relationships—all good things take effort. When we're younger, we think everything's going to be easy, but that's not the case. If, however, you have a really good life goal and a plan, and you keep yourself motivated, *that* is what leads to lasting success.

THE WRITING ON THE WALL

The first year I spent in Puerto Vallarta was dedicated to building up my team with Vacation Internationale. We were doing really great numbers, and eventually other companies moved to town and created more competition.

The owners of the company were getting older, and they started fighting about how aggressive they wanted to be in sales and growth. That discord filtered down to us, and we weren't sure what commitment they had. We had built up to a couple hundred people and all were depending on this job.

We all started looking around and saw that this opportunity might not last much longer. I asked myself, *What are my options?*

Before long, I went to work for another company, out of Nevada, that opened up an oceanfront condo building in the town of Puerto Vallarta. The owner had four stories of condos with a parking lot below, and he wanted to sell them as vacation ownership.

As tourism continued to grow, this business also did well. People had an open mind about fractional ownership because it felt like a lower risk to just buy a week or two, rather than making a big investment in a full-time place to live in Mexico.

I worked with this company for about 6 months, happy with the money I was making, until one day my boss called me into his office. He was there with the general manager out of Las Vegas. He said, "We're being audited by the main company, and we need you to sign some receipts."

I asked him, "What are you talking about?"

"Well," he told me, "to be honest with you, we've been charging the company more for your pay than we've been paying you. We just need you to sign these receipts saying you received the higher amount so the audit checks out."

They were smiling at me, and I just stared at them. "I can't sign those receipts." I said, "I never got that money!"

"Let's put it this way, if you want to keep your job, you're gonna sign 'em."

Moments like these are when you really learn about your character. It's easy to tell people who you are, but how are you going to react when something actually happens, spur of the moment, with no notice?

I was a little shocked when I heard myself say, "Listen, I'm not going to sign it. If you want to pay me the money, great, then I will. Otherwise, I can't sign something that's not true."

"Your choice," the general manager said. "You're fired. Get the hell out of here."

I left the office and walked through the parking lot, my world spinning. I had just started to accumulate some decent money. I had bought a nice, white, soft-top Jeep. Fifteen minutes earlier, I had shown up ready to work all day, and now I was walking out after being asked to commit fraud.

As I crossed the street, a guy came up to me. I thought he was a tourist until he said, "Excuse me, do you have a moment? I've been hired by the company to watch what's going on. Can we talk over a cup of coffee?"

When we sat down at the coffee shop, he introduced himself and told me that he was an investigator for the company out of Las Vegas, who hired him to look into what was going on with their properties. He asked me what happened at that meeting, and I told him, "They put me in a situation I couldn't agree to, and then they fired me."

He said, "You have a strong character. Most people probably would have just done what they asked. Let me give you some advice: in these kinds of situations, **Believe nothing of what people tell you and only half of what you see**, because that's usually what you'll end up with." Then he shook my hand and walked away.

I use this rule even today when I'm looking at a new opportunity…

That's a great golden rule for when people try to pitch you stuff, and it's one I've used my entire life.

That was also when I realized I was done working to make other people money. It was time to start working for someone I knew I could trust: myself.

CHAPTER 4

BUILDING A UNIQUE PARTNERSHIP IN PUERTO VALLARTA

I was twenty-five years old, and I was ready to be in business for myself. *I was going to be my boss!*

I decided to stay in Puerto Vallarta, and I partnered up with two of the people I had worked with at Vacation Internationale: Fernando Gonzales, who had worked in administration/sales management at the Mazatlan resort before coming to Puerto Vallarta, and Luz Maria, a woman I'd worked with in Puerto Vallarta, where she was a manager in administration/marketing, and who I'd been dating for the past year. (Almost forty years later, it's still the three of us!)

I had met one of the owners of La Fabrica de Francia—a furniture store from France that was popular throughout Mexico and had become the biggest department store in Mexico City—

and convinced them to sell their eight-bedroom mansion in the high-end area of Puerto Vallarta as a vacation ownership. Luz Maria and I were dating and working together at the time, and Fernando just so happened to be in town from Mazatlan and asked what we were doing. When we told him, he immediately said, "Let's do something together."

I had only been in Puerto Vallarta for a little over a year, so I hadn't had to set up a business in Mexico before and didn't know the process for administration, accounting, etc., but I knew how to sell to American clientele. Fernando had experience in administration. He knew the basics of the business, and he spoke English very well, so our skills complemented each other.

The three of us were still talking about that deal, trying to figure out what the next move was, when we began exploring other opportunities to work for ourselves.

One day, we were driving down the main road of Puerto Vallarta, just outside of town, when we saw a crane at a building site in the hotel zone. We went to look closer and saw that it was a small project, a condo hotel. One building was already built and the second building was going up. It was a six-story property, not on the ocean but with a sidewalk path to the beach, and with a restaurant on site.

We discovered they were trying to sell condos at full price, and we asked to speak with the owner. That's when we met Graziano Sovernigo.

We approached him, told him about the vacation ownership

we'd been doing, and said, "We'd like to buy twenty condos from you."

We hadn't looked for the financing yet and didn't have any financial plans, but Graziano's interest was piqued. He asked to see what we'd been doing so he could understand it better. A couple days later, we picked him up and brought him to the resort, where he could see that we had some success and that there was a lot of activity and sales happening.

A couple of weeks later, we met with Graziano again, and he told us, "This is the deal: you're going to sell this fractional ownership, and you're going to get your sales commission. I'm going to build the condos, and you're going to pay me the price I would get if I sold the condo to a full-time owner. If there's any money leftover in the middle, we'll split it, fifty-fifty."

We knew we could get 30 percent to 40 percent profit over full ownership, so we were in. We formed an independent sales company called The Villa Group. Fernando and I went up to Los Angeles, California, to meet with attorneys to structure our company. Graziano was very specific about how the company should be structured, so it would be both legal and credible.

From there, everything really started to flow.

That first project, Villa Del Mar, had 120 units, and we sold all of them within three years. We were doing incredible numbers and experiencing exponential growth, going from working for the previous company to now being partners in our own company and making significantly more money. Our fifty-fifty split was turning into millions of dollars.

MY MENTOR, GRAZIANO

I learned so much just by observing Graziano and getting to work with him.

Graziano had a unique story. He was originally from Northern Italy, but he and his three brothers immigrated to Canada after their town was destroyed during World War II. Once they got to Vancouver, they started a swimming pool company, which was very successful.

Ultimately, Graziano decided to leave Canada's cold, rainy weather. He said it was because it had rained for forty days and forty nights, which he took as a sign from God that it was time to leave. He moved to Puerto Vallarta, where we met him, when he was in his mid-forties. He became my true mentor, the person who really taught me a lot of the valuable lessons I've learned in my career, which contributed to my becoming a successful businessperson in today's world.

Graziano's style of working was that the day was for work and the night was for meetings. He was always a worker, and he loved it. If you drove into the resort and saw some gardeners working on the side of the road, wearing shorts and a hat—one of them would have been Graziano. (Once I came to our second resort and saw plants growing on the roof. I asked Graziano about them, and he said, "Oh, those are tomatoes. We're growing them for the restaurant.")

We were *always* busy, and we were making more money than we'd ever had in our lives.

Once we started making good money consistently, Fernando and

I decided to go out and buy ourselves gold Rolexes. We were delighted with our new status symbols, flashing them in each other's faces and feeling like big shots.

That night, we went to a meeting with Graziano. He looked at the ostentatious new watches on our wrists with disgust.

"You guys are idiots," he said. "You know, that kind of money can be reinvested in the business, where it can make a lot more money for you, instead of wasting it on stupid. expensive watches. Don't bring those damn things to work again."

Those watches didn't seem so shiny and exciting anymore, and we never wore them to work after that—only when we went out to the clubs.

A different night, shortly after we first opened up the business, we went out to dinner at La Perla, a high-end, fine dining restaurant at the Camino Real hotel, which was the first five-star chain in tourism in Mexico. The restaurant had flambe coffees, chateaubriand, and Caesar salads made right at your table. We had never seen that before; we thought it was so unique and special.

At that dinner, Graziano said, "Listen, I have something I want to ask you. You don't have to answer me now, but I'd like an answer by next week."

We were all intrigued. "Okay," we said, "what is it?"

Then Graziano asked one of the most important questions of my life, "Would you rather be a lion just for one day, or would you rather live your life as a sheep?"

What the heck kind of question is that? I wondered. But we'd promised to give our answer to Graziano in a week, so I spent the next few days thinking about it.

It was a question that the more you thought about it, the more the idea felt real and important, so I went back to Graziano and told him candidly, "I'd rather live one day as a lion."

Having thought about that question for decades, I now understand the unique mentality that comes from people who answer as I did. If you live like a lion, as though you only have that one day, it affects how much energy you put into what you do. It forces you to confront, "What do you want to experience?" And then go out and *have that experience.*

I've lived every day as a lion, and that mindset has lasted me a lifetime. (Recently, Fernando and I went to a business workshop in Cabo where we were all split up into different teams and seated at different tables. Each table had to choose an animal to represent them—six were lions, and one was a wolf. Maybe it's the type of people in my business, but I'm surrounded by lions!)

IT TAKES DISCIPLINE

One of the most important lessons I had already learned, but which working with Graziano heightened, was how to have discipline.

I had the discipline to take advantage of the opportunities I saw and not let them slip away. I still have that discipline today, and I'm still riding that same opportunity.

But I wasn't born with the discipline I have now. Part of my education process was watching to see what the people who had what I wanted did. Then, I had to provide a service to get paid, and I had to work to a point where I could make the money I wanted to make from the services I provided.

The first layer of discipline in your life is learning that nobody else is coming to help you. Then you have to add the layer of learning how to take care of yourself financially. The next layer is to know how to motivate yourself to achieve your goals instead of just wishing for them to come true. Each layer you add makes you more serious and more determined.

What kind of car do you want? What kind of house do you want to live in? How much money do you want to have in the bank?

Well, to get any of those, you have to create a business plan that involves getting paid for the services you provide.

Get Rich In Spite of Yourself says that the number-one rule for success is, "Whosoever will be great among you, let him minister unto the people's needs. And whoever the chief among you, let him give service in that field in which he is most skilled."

If you want to be the best in your field, you have to be the most skilled. You determine what you're most skilled at by what people are willing to pay you more for.

The book also says, "One cannot drive himself to success. One must be driven by a dominant, consistent, and enduring emotion or mood."

My dominant emotion or mood is to see what I can truly accomplish in my life. I want to keep life interesting, to keep it a journey, and to stay on the positive side. I am successful because I deliver a product that people really like.

> It's important to have discipline in your thinking too. The book *The Power of Your Subconscious Mind* taught me that your subconscious mind never shuts off. It's on 24/7, and sometimes it comes up with all these stupid thoughts. Once you understand that, though, you can discover that changing those thoughts is just like changing the channel on the TV. If something negative comes into your mind, simply change the channel and focus on something positive. Change your thoughts; don't let the negativity influence you.

I have always been the first one at work in the morning. After discovering I had the discipline to run a company, I wanted to create a foundation with my business so other people could come in and be successful, to create a stable environment where people can work and grow. That is still my goal today.

BECOMING A BETTER MANAGER

Every day I went to work with a purpose, with the strength and determination to make something happen, never just going through the motions. We worked ten-hour days, seven days a week, for two or three years. The opportunity was so good, we didn't want to miss out on a moment.

I still remember the day when my investment bank account had $1,000,000.00 US dollars in it…

By that point, we weren't just selling vacation ownership. We became resort owners and developers. After we did our first project, we bought the land next door, right on the ocean. Within the first ten years, we built our second resort in Puerto Vallarta called the Villa del Palmar, and sold all four hundred units.

I had to learn how to own restaurants, develop resorts, and get into that type of management, of being in charge of a lot of people. It was always exciting, but also a lot of work.

I didn't just achieve my own goals; I looked at the goals of the whole group and based my strategy on that. I put a lot of time and effort into being the best manager, with the best ideas. That was probably 50 percent more work than if I had just done the baseline required for that job, but I did the extra work because I wanted to keep growing and become a specialist at what I did.

I don't remember one manager I worked for who made a commitment to do the job well. They were just working for the paycheck. So when I became a manager, I took it more seriously—and I treated people how I wanted to be treated. I tried to educate people so they could move up and eventually replace me someday (a strategy we'll talk about more later!).

The book *The One Minute Manager* by Ken Blanchard and Spencer Johnson helped me change my management style. Many managers get into the habit of saying, "Hey, come here, you're doing this wrong." But people shut down their minds when all they hear is negatives.

Instead, I learned to first find something people are doing right and compliment them. "Gosh, I see you doing this great today, congratulations!" That's going to open up their mind so they're receptive to what you have to say next. Who doesn't want to hear more compliments? They're automatically going to lean in. Then you can follow it up with, "Hey, but I also saw this, and let me show you what you can be doing better."

I accepted the responsibility of the job. We lived in a party town, and a lot of the people who worked with me, who also had responsibilities, didn't know what time to leave the disco at night so they could show up for work on time. Those kinds of things can ruin their opportunities. I would go out and have fun, but I was still the first one at work in the morning.

One night, we went out to a bar called Casablanca for cocktails after dinner. Casablanca was like a Señor Frog's kind of place; the friendly bar in the middle of town where everyone went to have fun. Two American guys who were in sales came to Mexico and partied nonstop. One of them got drunk, fell, and cut himself on his arm. He didn't do anything about it for days and just kept partying. A couple of weeks later, he had to go to the hospital in Guadalajara because the cut got infected with gangrene and he ended up losing two fingers. What a waste!

GROWING UP

Graziano, Fernando, Luz Maria, and I kept working full time, and we all complemented each other's work. More companies started coming into Puerto Vallarta. There was more growth, which meant more competition. You could add up all the companies in town and multiply by ten, and they still wouldn't even get close to what we were doing. Mexico had a lot of tax structures for companies that invested in tourism, so we were able to take advantage of those benefits.

We were passionate people, and we had meetings all the time. I was a lion, and I wasn't going to be treated like a sheep at those meetings—even though some people will still try to treat you that way. I'd always have to stand up for myself. Graziano and Fernando already had a family so if we'd get into an argument, they'd say, "I have a family to take care of," or, "I have kids to support, so we have to do it this way."

I lost those arguments all the time. But then, when I was twenty-nine, Luz Maria and I got married in Puerto Vallarta, and everyone from the company came to our wedding. A lot of us were settling down and having kids. My daughter Brenda was born the next year. The timing felt right—I was more mature, I had a good job, and I was in charge of my life.

The business was so big and demanding, because starting a business from scratch is like having a baby! It needs so much. It was definitely a challenging couple of years. But it was stable by the time we had our daughter, and things were good.

Getting married and having kids actually helped me in business. When you have kids, it becomes more serious, because you have to provide for them. It also gave me a deeper purpose of why I wanted to be successful.

Then my second daughter Rebecca was born, and soon I was able to build a big mansion on the beach in Nuevo Vallarta, just north of Puerto Vallarta. It was a beautiful, ten thousand-square-foot house with marble floors and huge chandeliers. Looking back on it now, it was probably something like what a narco would have, but at the time I was what you called the "new rich."

After we built it, my mother and father came to visit us. When my father walked in, instead of being happy for my success, he said, "You can't show this to any of your siblings or even tell them about it. They would be very mad at you for having all this."

My mom, though, was so proud. She would stop and talk to the people walking on the beach and say, "My son owns this house, you know."

I was starting to make big money, which meant I had to learn how to take care of that money.

As the only American in the group, my financial situation was a little different than everyone else's. And, as we made more money, it was different than I had ever experienced. There were a couple of years in Hawaii where I hadn't even made enough money to file a tax return.

My friend Greg worked for Shearson Lehman as a stockbroker, so I asked his advice. He told me to see an international accounting firm, so I went to Laventhal and Horowitz in downtown San Diego. That's where I met Ashok Skripathi, who helped do my taxes.

I asked him, "I'm working in Mexico, and I live outside the US—do I have to file taxes?"

"Yes, you do," Ashok told me. "You're what's called an expatriate, because you live and work outside of the country, but you're an American citizen. That means you have to pay federal taxes. You don't have to pay state taxes, and you do get a deduction as an expatriate, but you do still have to pay federal taxes."

"I don't get it," I said. "Why do I have to pay taxes? I don't live in the United States, so I don't use any of the services those taxes pay for."

"Do you want to have credit one day?" he asked. "Do you want to buy a house and have a mortgage? Do you want to utilize any of these types of benefits from banking? Well, all of your financial information comes off your tax returns. Plus, let's say you get successful and you didn't declare your income—then you can't show the money anywhere, and you have to hide it. Is that the way you want to live your life?"

That was something to think about. I paused for a moment and then said, "Shit, no, I don't want to live that way. Okay, if I have to pay taxes, I'll just have to build that into my business plan."

Then Ashok said something that has stuck with me ever since. "Let me educate you: the US wants its tax money from its citizens, so you're going to have to pay taxes, no matter what. The best way to look at it is that the money you actually make is just whatever is left over after you pay taxes."

(Yes, I *also* had to pay taxes in Mexico, as anyone living and working there would.)

I've come to see that Ashok was correct. That's the only way to look at it. I've paid my share for many, many years now. These days, my US tax returns are about three and a half inches thick every year!

FINDING MY BALANCE

It took me a little while to get used to being a resort owner and developer. It felt like I had two different personas—my past and my present—and they stayed separate, never merging. If I thought about where I came from, I lost confidence, thinking, *Who am I? What do I think I'm doing?* In fact, back then, if anybody asked where I was from, I'd answer, "New York." That was a lot easier, and it made it seem like I came from a big city; that I was more sophisticated than I was.

Then I started reading about Edison and other great people who came from nothing and made something of themselves. America celebrates people who start on the bottom and work hard to end up on top. I kept reminding myself of those success stories, to change the channel on my thinking. I came to realize that, past or present, I was just *me*. Why not *me*?

During this time, I continued working with—and learning from—Graziano. We worked together for about ten years. During that time, he made a lot of money and worked ten hours a day, but he never took a day off until he eventually got Alzheimer's and was forced to stop working.

He definitely lived by the saying, "Dance while the music is playing, because you don't know when it's going to stop." We've all seen people who have had some success, but then it dries up. And so for years, we worked, worked, worked while the music was playing. It was great, but then I looked around and said, "What happens if the music plays for the rest of my life?"

For everything Graziano taught me about being a successful businessman—how to manage money, how to manage my ego, how to build a successful business in a structural way—I also saw that he never took a day off. He built a golf course in Nuevo Vallarta, and he never played it once. He had all these boats and a yacht marina, but he never took a day to go fishing—not one day.

Living with that dedication and restriction gave me a maturity about being in business. But I also learned about balance from seeing what Graziano modeled and deciding not to be exactly the same. I learned to work hard, yes, but I made time for the rest of my life too: to take vacations and to spend time with my family. It didn't take away from my business. In fact, it made me *better*, especially in the resort industry.

When I took vacations, I would go to other resorts around the world to evaluate what they were doing, and I always came back with ideas, something to change, or new details to add.

When you're doing the same job over and over again, you stop seeing the little things and lose track of the details. I call this motion sickness because you're just going through the motions of your job.

I counteracted that motion sickness by taking vacations and coming back with new inspiration to keep us current and modern. We were growing and I was learning these different areas I had to manage; my work kept feeling new and exciting too.

That's when we decided to expand our business into a new resort destination.

CHAPTER 5

WINS AND LOSSES IN CABO SAN LUCAS

After twelve or thirteen years of great success in Puerto Vallarta, my partners and I felt that it would be good to grow our business to include another destination that would create more value for the company.

We had heard a lot about a town called Ixtapa, near Zihuatanejo, south of Puerto Vallarta. Ixtapa was a growth town that the government was investing in as a tourism zone. We went there for a few days to check it out. I knew a couple of guys who were living there, and we all went to a disco called Christine's, which was one of a chain of discos in Mexico. We had a lot of fun on that visit, and we thought Ixtapa would be the next place for us to open a resort.

Two weeks later, however, Mexico had its worst earthquake in a hundred years, just off the coast of Ixtapa, and the town was destroyed. We went back again, and a lot of the hotels we had looked at were now just rubble.

After that, still searching for a place to expand, my partner Fernando said, "Hey, man, you gotta look at this place called Cabo. It looks really interesting. Let's fly over there so you can see it."

So I went with him to Cabo, and there was nothing there. I mean, absolutely nothing. Just the Giggling Marlin bar, El Squid Roe, and three or four hotels. Walking around town, we mostly saw drunk fishermen, not the tourists we were used to seeing in Puerto Vallarta. Back then, Cabo was a small fishing town with a drinking problem.

John Wayne actually put Cabo on the map because he would fly down there to go sport fishing. The Bisbee fishing tournament also began there. It's now a huge tournament with over ten million dollars in prize money, but back then it was twenty or thirty boats, mainly from California, and some diehard fishermen.

> Sammy Hagar also went to Cabo on vacation, staying at the Twin Dolphin, because his music hero Keith Richards of the Rolling Stones had gotten married there.

While Cabo didn't seem like a very pretty place, it did have a certain vibe. People called it Lands End, where the land meets the ocean. And in those places—also found in Kauai and Sedona, Arizona—an energy vortex is created.

I asked Fernando, "What do you see in this place?"

"*Potential*," he answered. "This company in Puerto Vallarta is opening up a place here, and I think they need some help."

"I'm not interested," I told him. "I want to take some time off and spend more time in San Diego."

Life was changing. None of us in our partnership had grown up with money, and now we actually had some. I was thirty-eight and had 20 million dollars in the bank—all legal and protected—so I didn't want to have to work as hard. I'm a hard worker with a strong work ethic, and I'd been building marketing programs and working with people for twenty years. I was kind of burned out and wanted to stay more on the development team and less on the marketing side.

By that point, Luz Maria and I had our second daughter, Rebecca. I bought a house in San Diego, and the four of us would go up there to escape the hot Mexican summer. We took hot air balloon rides, went out to eat at amazing restaurants, and visited the Del Mar racetrack. I would read the book and study the jockeys and horses, and my daughters would pick their favorites based on the name of the horse or color of the jockey's uniform. I would place our bets, and they ended up winning more than me! We had a really fun time.

There was a moment when I wanted to move up there permanently, but my oldest daughter, Brenda, said, "Nope. My friends are here in Puerto Vallarta, and I'm not leaving!"

FIRST IMPRESSIONS OF CABO

Although I didn't see the potential in Cabo then, Fernando was still interested and wanted to look for land to buy.

We found a property that looked promising and went for a tour. While we were there, I walked out on the beach and looked over to see a guy digging a hole in the sand. It looked like he was burying a body!

I grabbed one of the security guards and we went down there to see what was happening. When we got closer, we could see that this guy was burying a girl up to her neck in the hot sand.

She didn't look scared, and she wasn't screaming or anything, so we asked, "Hey, man. What's going on here?"

The guy stopped digging and said, "My name's Neil Stryker. I'm a third-generation Jewish priest and a holistic healer from Los Angeles. I bring various clients from Hollywood down here to detox. The hot sand helps sweat out all the body's impurities."

I got to know him as time went by, and it turned out that the girl in the sand was Paul Mitchell's girlfriend—the guy from the hair products and Patron tequila!

That was one of my first impressions of Cabo's wild energy. I called it the untamed Wild West at that time. In my first years in town, there was one grocery store that only received one delivery of supplies each week. Word spread quickly through town when the groceries came in, and two or three days later everything would be gone.

In our first couple of weeks there, we went to this little outdoor barbecue restaurant named Bad Company, where you could see the ocean from the patio. It only had one restroom, so everyone lined up for it, and women used the toilet while guys used the urinal right next to it. I've never used the same bathroom as a girl anywhere else I've ever traveled!

We also went to the Giggling Marlin, which was a fisherman's restaurant where they would tie fishermen upside down next to a picture of a marlin, so it looked like the marlin caught the human. That night, OJ Simpson was there, sitting in a booth in the corner with his girlfriend, his ex-wife, and their kids. They looked like they were having a great time. A week later, he was arrested for murder.

Cabo just had that kind of vibe!

I was on the journey of life—from Rhode Island, to Hawaii, then to Puerto Vallarta, which had been an amazing adventure for so many years—and I was ready for a completely new experience. But I didn't know yet what to expect from Cabo. There were only seven thousand people living there at the time. (Now, just twenty years later, there are 260,000, and it is Mexico's second most popular travel destination, after Cancun.)

We found a piece of property. Graziano came over to look at it, and we all agreed to purchase it. We got plans and permits and started to build.

That's when we learned that our property had some history behind it. The property—which was on Cabo Bay, where the weather can get violent—was on a sand dune. Unbeknownst to us when we bought it, the Indians who used to live in the mountains above the bay hundreds of years ago would bury their dead in the dunes and let the sand clean the bones. Then they would go down, get the bones, and bring them back up to the mountains. After we started building, we found some bones, which was kind of scary.

LIFE CHANGES

We built the first phase of the project in Cabo, called the Villa del Palmar Cabo. The town was still empty. There was not a lot of tourism, which meant there was big money to be made… eventually. I mostly stayed in Puerto Vallarta or at our house in San Diego.

Then Luz Maria and I started growing apart. Although we were equal partners in the business, we didn't want the same things in life anymore. She wanted to travel to Europe and see the world, after growing up with no vacations, like me. I wanted to stay in San Diego, to be back in the US after all those years and get back to the American lifestyle.

After about a year, we separated. The kids still went to school in Puerto Vallarta, so Luz Maria stayed there with them.

Around that same time, about a year into our Cabo project, Graziano decided he wanted to build his own resorts without any partners. That left the three of us to buy him out—not just of the Cabo property but the entire company. We met the attorneys in LA and did a blind bid, and we won, but it cost us basically all of our money to buy Graziano out. (We shook hands and stayed friends for many years, though, and he helped us whenever we needed it.)

Graziano had this guy working in Cabo as a construction manager to oversee the project. He was doing a good job, but I came to find out that he had his wife there *and* he was dating our restaurant manager's wife on the side. Nobody knew about it until one night they just took off together. He left his wife there without telling her anything, and she left her husband, so it created a lot of drama—and we had nobody left to oversee the construction.

Without Graziano there to do all the construction and hotel management, I started going to Cabo more and more, getting more involved in everything. I had no other options; I had to do it.

It was exciting to be there doing something new, but life continued throwing more challenges my way. Cabo turned out to be the most extreme challenge of my life so far.

Fernando was still going back and forth between the resorts we had in Puerto Vallarta and our new project in Cabo, but he had three kids and he was settled in Puerto Vallarta; he had made the city of Puerto Vallarta his home. Just as the first phase in Cabo was basically done and ready to open, he came to town and told me, "I want out. You have to buy me out of the company."

"What are you effing talking about?" I said. "*How?* We have no money; I have no money; nobody is here for construction; no one for hotel management…The business is not doing well at all, and there's no way I can buy you out. What is happening?"

"Well, I've decided to get into politics, and I'm running for mayor of Puerto Vallarta. It's been a dream of mine for a long time, and with the new political system, I see an opportunity. So that's what I need to do, and that means I have to quit the company."

Of course, he ended up winning—Fernando became the mayor of Puerto Vallarta. He even brought me up on stage during his victory speech. I was the only American for miles. I remember sitting there, thinking, *What am I doing here?*

So then it was just me now in Cabo…

That was the first time I was alone. In Puerto Vallarta, I'd had Graziano in charge of construction, Fernando in administration and sales, Luz Maria in administration and marketing, and me in both sales and marketing. We had a really tight team running our company like a well-oiled machine for all those years, and then...it was all on me. When you have four people on your team, each doing something different, it's a lot easier than one person having to do it all in a problem environment.

All three of them were just gone, and I had to do it all myself. We were already committed. We had all our money in this project. It was either make it work...or fail completely and have to start over at square one.

> One thing to understand about doing business in Mexico at the time is that we couldn't just borrow money, because Mexican banks did not give loans for developments. We had to just build our business and keep working it until we found that sweet spot where it started making money—something I was glad I'd learned to do from Graziano.

Those first few months that I was in Cabo all by myself were the biggest challenge of my life. It was so stressful.

My daughters would come visit occasionally, but they had to go to school back in Puerto Vallarta. When I talked to them on the phone, they would cry and ask me, "Daddy, where are you? Are you going to come home tonight?" It was heartbreaking.

And then my father died.

We never, even as I was an adult, had a conversation about life or anything, which is so weird to me now, as a father of four. My son and I are best friends! I could never imagine not being involved in their lives.

When he died, it was not a shock—he had had a heart attack and a quadruple bypass when he was sixty-five, was on every med you can think of, and his life deteriorated quickly after that—because I didn't actually know the man that well.

I took a trip back to Rhode Island to help take care of my mom, and she made me buy her a coffin so she'd be ready when her time came. I helped her rearrange the house and clean out the basement and the garage. One of my sisters and her two kids lived in the apartment upstairs, so they were close by and helped take care of her day to day.

I'd go back to visit her two or three times a year, but during this time it felt like everything was going wrong all at the same time. I tried to move the needle as much as I could with everything I had to do, but the pressure was so intense, and I didn't know how I would take it.

A TIME OF LEARNING

George Harrison said that he quit the Beatles because there was so much stress that he felt like his insides were being peeled back, layer by layer like an onion, all the way down to his core. Some days, I felt that way too. The stress was just too much; I felt like it was peeling something away inside me as well.

When that feeling threatened to overwhelm me, I'd go to my room, lie on the couch, and listen to classical music to try to calm down.

I also learned a lot about myself during this time period. You never really know who you are until you are put through extreme stress. The person with the big mouth who is always in everybody's face may turn out to be the first one to run away from any problems, while the person who is quieter and more passive may be the one to run into a burning building. You just never know.

I certainly hadn't known about myself that I would have such strong determination and will to succeed. I learned that I could handle the stress. I could deal with the pressure. I could make the right decisions and do what needed to be done. Business doesn't depend on luck, good or bad; a business is the accumulation of making a series of right decisions—decisions that were now all up to me to make. I knew that my work ethic would create my luck, and that once I could get some momentum going in a positive direction, more good things would follow.

I had already built the practice of starting each day with a positive thought, and I leaned into that. Every morning, no matter how bad things were around me, I wouldn't get out of bed until I could think of something positive. ("I'm alive, I'm awake, I feel great!")

That's also when Plan E really came alive and was tested. Before that, we had all these business plans and I had other people to lean on when making decisions. In Cabo, though, things weren't working out how I'd planned. Maybe if we had stayed together as a company, if we hadn't spent so much money to buy out Graziano, if Fernando hadn't gone into politics, if Luz Maria and I hadn't ended our relationship—maybe if all these things had been different, my time in Cabo would have been easier.

That wasn't how things worked out, though. So I had to start tweaking my plans, keeping what did work and then trying something new, over and over, until things started moving in the right direction again.

Plan A hardly ever works—the idea may have been good, but maybe the execution was horrible—and when that happens, it's very emotional. You go through a progression of thoughts, from *I'm stupid*, to, *How could this happen to me?*

Fortunately, however, I was able to keep going until I got to a plan that worked. Knowing that Plan A rarely goes as planned, I was able to stay energized rather than wasting time thinking, *Poor me. Why is this happening to me?*

I also realized I was fighting with myself every day, wondering, *Why am I doing this stressful job?*

Then I had a good talk with myself and said, "Accept this is the job you're going to do or move on to something else."

Well, I decided to keep working and things became much better because I wasn't losing all that energy every day fighting with myself, and instead I was committed to my job.

I didn't waste all that emotional energy worrying about whether or not my first idea was right. I could see the opportunity; I knew I just had to build up the team and the business to meet it. And if I went to work that day and the idea I had didn't work perfectly, I knew to keep going. It wasn't about me or whether I could do it or not—it was about how to just *get it done*.

If you find yourself in a similar situation, understand that starting your own business is an emotional time. Know that if you just keep working and trying to find a solution to the problem, and if you keep moving forward every day—even if it's just an inch at a time—sooner or later it's going to happen for you.

If you're starting at the bottom and want to get to the top, it's going to be a bumpy ride. People aren't going to be out there throwing money at you and saying, "You're amazing! Let me do this for you." That's not reality. Instead, recognize where you are and where you want to go. Keep making and tweaking your plans. Remember that this period won't last forever, and find something to help you deal with the stress you are experiencing.

When you're so stressed out, your body absorbs it back into itself. At night, I would come home and eat, and then I'd have nervous, jumpy sleep all night. I just couldn't relax because I kept thinking about what problem was going to happen next.

Eventually, I found some stress relief in moving my body. While I was in Cabo, I started playing tennis. I loved watching it on TV. The resort had tennis courts—they're practically mandatory at any resort in Cabo—so I started playing three times a week between four and six in the afternoon. After that, I'd go home, have a nice dinner, and all the stress had left my body so I slept great.

I also liked to walk or run on the beach in Cabo, as part of an exercise program I could really enjoy. (And I still enjoy running on the beach when I'm in town!) Running was an all-inclusive package to get rid of stress in my body and help my mind relax by meditating.

You have to complement your work life with taking care of

yourself. That's crucial to avoid burnout. And it's not about just doing one thing right; it's about doing a few things right; and your health is a big thing you want to get right. Eating healthy food, sleeping well, and getting exercise are critical to be able to work at an elite level. I'm happy I learned that early on because my body is still in good shape today.

I also bought a Harley-Davidson motorcycle, which I would ride out on the two-lane highway to Todos Santos, a small town about two and a half hours away. There were about fifteen of us who would get together to ride out on Saturdays, have lunch at Shut Up Franks, and then ride back. It was important to find something fun to do and to just get away from my problems for a while.

TAKING THE LEAP

The biggest thing I did to create a shift in my attitude was spontaneously going skydiving.

That first horrible year, I was in a really bad state of mind. I was getting divorced. I had no money. I was in the middle of nowhere, with no place to go and nothing to do. I needed an attitude adjustment.

One day, I was at the resort, right on the bay, and I saw some guys drift down from the sky and land next to us. I asked them what they were doing, and they said, "We're a skydiving company—we do it every afternoon."

I went back into our resort, found the hotel manager, Mario, and said, "Hey, I want you to come with me."

I didn't tell him where we were going, I just brought him with me to the little airport in Cabo, with a dirt runway and a Cessna plane. Mario looked around as we got onboard, and then we were flying up to 10,000 feet.

When the instructors started clipping onto us, to do tandem jumps since we were beginners, Mario finally asked me, "What are we doing?"

"We're going skydiving," I told him. "Don't worry about it; just enjoy it!"

When it was my turn to jump, I paused to look out the door of the airplane. I could see Cabo down below us. The cars looked like ants. I was nervous but excited. And then we jumped!

I screamed nonstop for the first ten seconds, letting out all my anger and frustration, sadness and fear, all the negative emotions that had been building up in me. I just let them go into the wind.

Then I pulled the chute, and we glided down, finally landing on the beach.

And that's all it took to change my whole attitude. I could see that things weren't really that bad—after all, I had just survived jumping out of an airplane. It was like I had cleansed myself of the funk I'd been in. Instead of looking at everything that was going wrong, I was ready to ask, "Okay, how can we start fixing things?"

Mario wasn't very happy with me, but it was still a great time! That shift, combined with making the right decisions, led to things starting to get better.

WHAT GOES DOWN MUST COME UP

Things started to shift quickly in Cabo.

Don Koll, a big developer out of Newport, California, came into town, bought the Palmilla resort, and opened a golf course. Seemingly overnight, we saw the whole demographics of Cabo change. Now, instead of the drunk fishermen, the town was full of golfers, tourists, and people on vacation from the US, especially Los Angeles—people with great jobs, who had money and wanted to spend it, buying houses or vacation fractionals.

We started seeing our business change, too. The resorts began filling up, and we started selling more. I could feel the shifting energy in the air. This became a big growth time in my life, both in business and in learning what I was made of.

With the uptick in sales, we started construction again and finished the first resort. A couple of years later, Fernando—who had become a federal Congressman in Mexico City and then lost a run for governor of the state of Jalisco—came back to work. I asked him, "If you had become governor, would you have ever come back?"

"Oh, no way," he told me. "I would have run for president!"

By then, the company was doing really well, and it was great timing because I needed him back to help with all the growth we were experiencing.

> I often had to have the same conversation each time I met someone new. They'd hear me speak and say, "Wait a minute, you're an American!"
>
> "Yeah," I'd say, "I am an American."
>
> "And you own and develop resorts in Mexico?"
>
> "Yes," I'd say, knowing what was coming next.
>
> Sure enough, "Are you a drug dealer?"
>
> The first thing people think when you're successful in Mexico is that you must be dealing drugs. I've been fighting that untrue stereotype for most of my adult life.

Sammy Hagar opened the Cabo Wabo Cantina, a tequila bar with a stage for musicians. He and I became good friends, and I got to hang out with the rock stars who came through town, like Van Halen and Guns N Roses. Hanging out with those guys could get crazy, but it was always fun.

> In fact, Sammy Hagar is still a good friend, and in 2021 he spent some time between Christmas and New Year's at my resort in Loreto.

Cabo was now popping! Tourism in Mexico was becoming a very strong business, with double-digit growth every year. I got along with our competitors in town, and we formed associations to guide the transformation of Cabo. We worked together with the community and other developers to put in money for more airlines to fly into Cabo. That led to a big influx of people and a really fun time managing the success of Cabo.

We had great numbers, and money coming in, so we decided to expand. When we were looking for property, we found this lot on the beach in Cabo San Lucas, owned by a development company, Situr. The property actually had three lots, but we were only interested in buying one. When we went to Mexico City to complete the transaction, the British guy who was representing the owner said, "You're only going to buy one lot, but I'm going to add the other two lots on this contract. You don't have to buy them; we just want to show this income on our financials for this year so our stock price goes up."

We were fine with that, as long as there was no recourse and we could walk away if we wanted. He said, "No problem," so we did it.

Situr ended up being investigated by the New York Stock Exchange. They crashed and burned, and we ended up keeping the other two properties for pennies on our dollar. It was something in our favor to have those three lots when Cabo started getting bigger! Those properties are now vibrant and successful, and we've since opened a fourth.

I watched Cabo grow in popularity, but to me it still felt like a small town—just a really busy small town! It had this great nightlife, and I invested in an Italian restaurant outside the resort, which became one of the top restaurants in Cabo. I'd go hang out there a few nights a week. And I'd end up seeing the same people everywhere—at restaurants, cocktail bars, and the disco. There was an eclectic group of us living in Cabo at the time.

In 2005, I opened up a bar called Desperados. A number of Rock and Roll Hall of Fame musicians have played there over the years—Billy Gibbons from ZZ Top, Robin Zander from Cheap Trick, Duff McKagan and some of the other guys from Guns N Roses, of course Sammy Hagar from Van Halen, Don Felder of the Eagles, Steve Steves from Billy Idol, and Johnny Lang. I always loved music, and this gave me the chance to meet all these musicians of the songs I grew up with. It was so much fun.

With the bar, I was also able to start throwing New Year's Eve parties. They weren't open to the public, so we could keep it smaller with just friends attending. We'd still have fifty or sixty people, and we'd have dinner, then the band would come out and play a show until midnight, when we'd toast and ring in the new year.

Those parties felt like a reward after working so hard and making it through those difficult times the first few years I was in Cabo.

Work is no fun if you don't reward yourself, and it's important to celebrate having a great year and doing a good job. Taking time off and doing something to enjoy the ride is part of having a long-term mentality. But you have to clearly and consciously build that into your plan, because if you don't, you're going to end up burning out, failing, and having to start again at the bottom.

If you could invite all the musicians you liked and see them in a live show at a bar you owned, wouldn't you leap at the chance?

FINDING LOVE AGAIN IN CABO

I even met my second wife in Cabo.

After we divorced, Luz Maria spent all of her extra time in Europe. She moved to Switzerland part of the time, and she took our daughters over there with her when they weren't in school. Her boyfriend was a big banker in Zurich, with all kinds of connections, and he was able to get them into a private summer camp in the Swiss mountains, called Camp Montana.

The first time they were going to camp, I told my daughters I would bring them and fly back home with them afterward. First, we went to New York City and saw Broadway shows. Then I took them to Lucerne and dropped them off at Camp Montana.

But I had no plans for the two weeks they were in camp.

I had been riding my Harley for a while at that time, and I was looking for a motorcycle tour while I was there. So the president of the Swiss chapter of Harley Davidson, Rudy, contacted me and said, "Hey, man, I have a restaurant in a ski area named Davos, but it's closed in the summer. I will personally take you on a Harley tour throughout Switzerland."

That was so incredible, I can barely put it into words. I met Rudy in Zurich, and he brought me to the Harley Davidson shop downtown where they had all brand-new motorcycles. We took off for two weeks, and he showed me all the best restaurants and hotels in Europe. We went through northern Italy and into the south of France, where the Tour de France was going on. We stayed at the Hotel de Paris Monte-Carlo—even though, at first, they didn't want to let us in the city because we were on motorcycles—and we had dinner at the amazing rooftop restaurant during Swiss day and ended up in the casinos that night.

I enjoyed myself so much, and I ended up doing that trip three times.

After a couple years in Cabo, I started dating again. It was kind of a shock to me—my parents were married for fifty years, so I never contemplated being divorced...and now here I was, back on the dating scene!

In my third or fourth year in Cabo, I went to a Halloween party. My friend and I were standing in a line at the bar that was six people deep. This cute blonde came out of the crowd and asked me, "Do you want me to get you a cocktail?"

I said, "Sure," and we started talking when she came back with my drink.

Jolene and I went on a date the next night, and we were together for eighteen years after that. What I didn't know that first night was that she actually worked for my company, in the guest services division. I had a rule against dating anybody I worked with, but we were a good size company with a few hundred people working for us by then, and I had never met her. A couple months later, her boss found out that she was dating me and said, "You're fired—there's no way the boss's girlfriend is working for me."

Four years after we met, we got married in Hawaii, on the island of Lanai. I always told myself that one day I would get married at sunset, barefoot on the beach, and that's exactly what we did.

We had two kids, Jewel and Owen. When my son was born, we found a house in Rancho Santa Fe, in San Diego, so we could be part of that school district, which was one of the best in California. Their home was there, but they grew up in Cabo.

Overall, I look back on my time in Cabo as an incredible experience. Today, Cabo is as big as Las Vegas and one of the top resort destinations in the world—and I can say that I'm one of its founders. Most importantly, the lesson I learned during the years I lived in Cabo—always believe in yourself, even when no one else does—has stayed with me the rest of my life.

CHAPTER 6

ALL MY LEARNING COMES TOGETHER IN LORETO

After my daughter Jewel was born in 2005, Fernando and I decided to each explore our own projects—a decision that I think ultimately saved our partnership, because it allowed us to have more freedom. Fernando developed projects in Cancun and on the other side of Puerto Vallarta, and I found a new direction to go in as well.

On weekends, my wife Jolene and I would take the car and go on road trips to explore the Baja peninsula. We listened to music and drove all around Baja, experiencing these unique small communities.

And that's how we found the little town of Loreto.

Loreto was founded by the king of Spain in 1620. It is a rural, agrarian community in the middle of the Baja Peninsula, and it's where the first Mission of the Californias was started. We stayed there one weekend, and I saw the beautiful mountains surrounding the turquoise Sea of Cortez with the most perfect, pristine bay—one of the nicest in all of Baja California. In the morning, when the sun comes up, everything glows red from the copper in the mountains. In the afternoon, they turn a rich shade of sparkling brown. The bay is part of a National Marine Park, and it is alive with nature. As I watched pelicans swoop down into the water, diving for bait fish, I understood why French diver Jacques Cousteau called Loreto "the natural entrance to the largest aquarium in the world."

It felt like Loreto combined aspects of every place I'd ever lived: the mountains of Puerto Vallarta, the land-meets-the-ocean energy of Cabo, and the breathtaking beauty of Hawaii.

I was impressed with what I saw, so I put out the word that I was interested in finding property there. I was told about a few options, so we went to tour those properties with a real estate sales guy who was a former Cabo beach seller. On our way to look at one property, we drove down a dirt road to the middle of nowhere and saw the perfect place to build a resort—right on the bay, surrounded by those beautiful mountains, and complete with an island view.

We were told that it had been owned by a doctor in La Paz who had unfortunately passed away and his wife was desperate to sell it. It was a big piece of property—perfect for me to develop—but the widow didn't know what to do with it. I came at just the right time to help her. Her husband had promised to take her to Hawaii one day, and I said, "Señora, you can now go." And she did, taking her two daughters with her on her dream trip to Hawaii.

When I bought the property, everybody back in Cabo thought I was crazy. They told me that Loreto was in the middle of nowhere and asked why I didn't go somewhere more popular. But I just felt comfortable there, and I trusted my own senses and life experiences. I knew what people liked when they went on vacation, and all the boxes were checked. I thought, *If someone builds a five-star resort here, people will love it." Why not me?*

And with the tremendous growth Cabo experienced, people in Mexico began to understand what tourism can do for the economic value of an area.

RECOGNIZING OPPORTUNITIES

In 2008, I was invited to play at Torrey Pines golf course a few days before the US Open was to take place there. I was partnered with the then-West Coast vice president of Bank of America. We got to talking and around the eleventh or twelfth hole he told me, "I meet a lot of developers who are very successful. They have a methodical approach to their jobs and their growth. But they all seem to have one thing in common: at the pinnacle of their success, when they're ready to take on the biggest project of their careers, they think their success is automatic and they quit doing the fundamental things they did to get to that point—and that's where I see most developers fail."

At the time, I didn't think much of his statement. I just thought, *Well, that's not me*, and kept playing. But a few days later, I woke up in the morning to his words still in my mind. *Oh my gosh*, I thought. *That actually does sound a lot like me right now.*

Where usually we developed our resorts in phases, rolling out one and having some success before moving on to the next, in Loreto I was ready to do everything all at once. But the more I thought about that banker's words to me, the more I realized... maybe that was a mistake.

So I decided to change my plans. I would just start with phase one of the resort. Then, if things kept going well, I'd move on to the next—just like we used to do.

Shortly after that, the Great Recession hit. Banks were closing. People were holding onto whatever money they had. Nobody was traveling. It was a really scary time for everybody. I was so thankful that I hadn't tried to do everything at once; that I didn't have all my money invested in a dead project.

In fact, during that time of the Great Recession, I was going to postpone building the resort. I had the design, permits, and everything ready to go when the recession hit, but every development that I knew about, anywhere, had shut down.

By this time, I was well known in Baja from all the construction we'd done in our resorts in Puerto Vallarta and Cabo. All these guys who had construction companies, electrical companies, and the like started contacting me because they were going to be shut down completely. There were absolutely zero projects coming in, and they wouldn't be able to survive. They said, "Señor Owen, listen. We will get materials at cost and work with no profit. You could save 30 percent to 40 percent on a construction project right now because nobody else is building anything. *And* you'll get all the best workers to come work with you."

I really started thinking seriously about it. Nobody knew what was going to happen as a result of this recession—if all the financial institutions disappeared, all my money would be worthless anyway—but I knew this wasn't humanity's last gasp. Slowly but surely, we would bounce back and then everybody would start going out again. If I saved a bunch of money building my resort now, I'd be sitting pretty by the time everyone was ready to start traveling and spending money again.

So I decided to do the project, and I did have all the best workers on it. I got great materials at a great price, and everyone worked so hard to make it incredibly beautiful. I got good quality furniture 60 percent off, because they wanted the sale to keep their factory open. I had Anderson windows and doors shipped all the way from the US, for a great deal, because they had no other jobs.

And a couple of years later, when the recession was over, the resort was finished, and I opened those doors. People came in at a trickle in the beginning, but little by little, they kept coming. Pretty soon I was 90 percent full year round and winning awards for my resort and golf course. A blogger came and called Loreto "the next best thing," telling his readers to visit us soon before it was packed all the time.

I look back now and realize that I made a great decision because I was able to control my fears and take advantage of the opportunity when it was presented to me.

SUCCESS = 90% PREPARATION + 10% OPPORTUNITY

You can't control when opportunity comes; you can only control how prepared you are for it when it does arrive.

Success, especially through growth, is 90 percent preparation and 10 percent opportunity. We all go through cycles in life, and during those cycles there is often a lot of downtime where nothing much is happening. But instead of being bored or waiting for the next stage of the cycle, where something exciting happens, you can use those downtimes to prepare yourself for the next level.

Even when things are good, look ahead and evaluate: what's the next thing you can prepare to shore up the foundation of your plans? What tools can you develop now that you may need in the future?

Many people wait for the opportunity to arrive and *then* start to prepare themselves, but they often miss the opportunity because they weren't ready for it. When you prepare yourself as much as possible ahead of time, you are always ready. You have more time to think about what is required when the situation arises. And you can have a plan in place to handle what is needed when the opportunity presents itself.

I survived and grew this way in Cabo and later in Loreto too. If I was going to design a resort with three buildings, I'd start by building one first, with the pool, restaurant, and public areas. Then I'd start marketing the hotel, get it growing, and sell some vacation ownership. Once that business got bigger and was on good footing, then I started the second phase. Same thing; once that phase is solid, then I could start the third.

That's how you prepare to grow, by being a strategic thinker. Keep one eye on today and one on the future.

But most people are held back from even considering an opportunity, let alone preparing for it, because of fear.

Fear stops 90 percent of people from doing something they may want to go for. A lot of people experience this throughout their careers and their lives. Your subconscious mind works by trying to help you think through, *Oh my gosh, what if all these things go wrong?* But as you think through all the worst-case scenarios, that fear freezes you in your tracks, so you don't make a move.

You have to overcome your fears in order to grow and prepare to take advantage of opportunities. Develop a process whereby you overcome your fears by analyzing things in their true form. Weigh the positives and negatives, and make your decisions based on that information. You have to take a little risk every once in a while, but it should be an *educated* risk.

This is exactly what I did when I decided to go ahead with building the resort in Loreto. I knew that the recession wouldn't last forever. It was two or three difficult years, and then things improved. But if I had waited those two years for things to get better and *then* started construction, I would be competing with all the new projects starting back up. All the commodities, materials, and labor prices would be way higher, and I'd have to fight to get good workers.

So I had to overcome my fears around the recession, analyze what was likely to happen, and take an educated risk.

And it turned out to be a good business decision.

WHAT'S THE WORST THAT COULD HAPPEN?

Some people may have thought that Loreto was my crisis time, but it wasn't. The first year of Cabo—that was crisis time, as was the beginning of the COVID-19 pandemic in 2020. Compared to those times, Loreto was easy. I knew what I wanted to do and had a picture in mind of exactly what would work. And because I had learned so much through trial and error, discovering Plan E, I wasn't worried about whether it was going to happen or not—I knew that it would.

To deal with the naysayers, I asked myself, "Well, what's the worst thing that could happen?"

I pictured building this gorgeous resort in the middle of nowhere, a place with no previous history of success, and then imagined what it would look like if no one showed up. In my mind, it was like *The Shining*, the movie with Jack Nicholson, where he has to take care of an isolated hotel in the wintertime and he goes crazy. Chasing my wife and kids around...If that was the worst that could happen to me, I was okay with that.

When you are evaluating a big decision, try to think through both the worst-case and best-case scenarios. Once you know both extremes—neither of which are likely to happen in the way you think—work through what's most realistically going to happen. This is likely somewhere in the middle, but doing this exercise allows you to think through as many possibilities as you can, so you can work through potential obstacles.

> You can also make a pro/con list, just as Benjamin Franklin used to do. Here is his advice, written in a letter to Joseph Priestley from September 19, 1772:
>
>> When these difficult Cases occur, they are difficult chiefly because while we have them under Consideration all the Reasons pro and con are not present to the Mind at the same time; but sometimes one Set present themselves, and at other times another, the first being out of Sight. Hence the various Purposes or Inclinations that alternately prevail, and the Uncertainty that perplexes us.
>>
>> To get over this, my Way is, to divide half a Sheet of Paper by a Line into two Columns, writing over the one Pro, and over the other Con. Then during three or four Days Consideration I put down under the different Heads short Hints of the different Motives that at different Times occur to me for or against the Measure. When I have thus got them all together in one View, I endeavour to estimate their respective Weights; and where I find two, one on each side, that seem equal, I strike them both out: If I find a Reason pro equal to some two Reasons con, I strike out the three. If I judge some two Reasons con equal to some three Reasons pro, I strike out the five; and thus proceeding I find at length where the Ballance lies; and if after a Day or two of farther Consideration nothing new that is of Importance occurs on either side, I come to a Determination accordingly.

I knew I could make things work in Loreto, and I was very confident this location would be successful. I just had to keep putting together all the pieces I'd learned from previous experience.

Once again, I was doing it on my own, but I had learned from my time in Cabo. I knew what to do while overseeing construction and getting airlines to add more flights so people could make it to the town. It was certainly a challenge, but there was no faking it and no luck involved; I had to rely on my experience and commitment to success.

But sometimes even those skills were seriously challenged.

The whole time I was building this property in Loreto, anyone coming in or out had to take a long, winding back road through an arroyo, because the property wasn't connected to the highway. The problem was, there was another property standing between mine and the highway, and I'd need to buy part of that property to connect my resort with the highway 1 and make a proper entrance to a three-thousand-acre development.

The family who owned that property next to mine was from Hermosillo. For two years I tried to get them to sell me a piece of her property, so we could connect directly to the main highway, but they didn't respond to my calls, emails, or texts. They didn't even respond when I sent an attorney to make them a proposal—*nothing*.

Then one day, shortly after I opened the resort, when they *still* had not responded, I just got *so mad*. When I went back to San Diego that weekend, I punched out a scathing email to them, and it was the worst email I've ever written to this day. I called them an uneducated ranchero—the worst insult you can call somebody in Baja—and said that they were too stupid to recognize that if my property did well, their lot was going to increase in value too. This should have been a no-brainer for them!

The next day, I completely regretted sending that email. *Owen, that was so stupid*, I thought. *Why did you do that? They are going to be so insulted now, you're never going to get your road built!*

The day after that, however, I got the shock of my life: an email back from them, saying, "Okay, send me the plans for the property and we'll make a deal."

That was the missing part of this project, and once I had that, it all came together.

The deal went through, and I carved out the road, undergrounding the utilities and paving the way right from the highway to the front door of my resort, which is now only about twenty minutes from the Loreto International Airport.

Success!

A HOLE IN ONE

Loreto was also where I opened my first golf course.

After Don Kole, a developer out of Newport Beach, had come to Cabo and built his golf course, I saw the demographics there change from drunk fishermen to golfers with money, and I credit that shift with the building-up of Cabo. There are now twenty-two golf courses in Cabo—more than in Las Vegas or anywhere else in North America.

Knowing who your demographics are for marketing is 90 percent of the preparation needed to have a successful outcome. When we experienced this growth in the Cabo market, I knew that I wanted to get the golfer demographic to come to Loreto as well; it was part of our master marketing plan. Not only did I have this very picturesque piece of property for a resort, but I also had enough property in the development for a fractional ownership project and houses there. But first, if I wanted golfers to come, I had to develop a golf course!

So I went on a quest of finding an architect I wanted to work with. I finally found Reese Jones, who I learned about from the 2008 Open in San Diego, and we collaborated for close to three years on the design before starting construction. We both agreed that golf courses were getting too difficult for the average recreational player; this was part of the reason for the decline in golf's popularity.

Developing this empty piece of land has been one of the most enjoyable projects I have done so far. It's been amazing to watch it take shape and to create a unique experience for our guests.

Even before it opened, I started heavily promoting the golf course to build up momentum. I invited golf writers and pros to come play for a weekend, during which Don Felder of the Eagles came and played. (There was a rumor that this is where the Eagles wrote the song "Hotel California," so who better to invite than Don, who co-wrote that song!)

The vice president of the Tournament Players Club, or TPC, a brand that has some of the nicest courses on the PGA Tour, emailed me to say they were interested in making my course part of the TPC network—and it would be the first TPC course outside the United States. I assumed it must be really expensive to join this exclusive network, so my email back to them was very nice in expressing my regret in having to pass on the opportunity: "I'm just opening up now, so I don't have the revenue to pay for your brand. Maybe I can take advantage of this offer in a couple years."

They replied and asked if they could come down to talk to me and do a presentation. Of course I said yes.

About a month later, the vice president of the PGA Tour came down to Loreto, along with one of the press guys who had been there for our invitational weekend. They said they'd heard about my course from a lot of people, and that it was exactly the type of course they wanted in their portfolio. They even showed me the logo they'd created, adding their brand to mine, and it looked amazing. (They had me at the logo!)

I told them again, "I'd love to do this. Having a brand like yours and being part of your site would definitely make us stand out. It would be amazing for us, but I'm just opening up. There's no way I can afford it."

But they told me, "Listen, we want this golf course in our portfolio, and we're willing to make a deal you need to do in order to get this done."

I am a marketer, and I was talking to a PGA pro about having our course logo on the color of his shirt...this deal was the best thing we could have done at this time of the development.

We agreed on an amount, did the deal, and that put the TPC's stamp of approval on my course—still the only TPC course outside the United States. And it's a big deal. Golfers come here from all over the world just to play the course. We have won awards for being one of the top courses in North America and in the world.

Even better, my son now plays golf for his high school team. We love playing together. Whereas in most team sports the parent has to just sit on the sideline, we are able to practice together while spending four or five hours together too.

EXPANDING LORETO

My resort in Loreto is a resounding success, and I finished phase two even during a pandemic.

We have won the "World Travel Award" for the best beach resort in Mexico and Central America for seven years in a row.

Previously, the tourism demographics we implemented appealed to the golf, retirement, and adventure travel communities, but now we're seeing them shift more to families. As such, I'm preparing for the future of Loreto with a master-planned community built on seven beachfront lots. Plenty of development to keep me occupied for years!

I bought property that is going to be full service, both condominiums and a resort, mixed-use residential and tourist area. I'm also selling vacation ownership and 140 houses. In 2021, I saw a 110 percent increase in revenues over 2020.

And my success hasn't been only financial.

Recently I was having dinner at one of the restaurants at the resort when a couple came up to me and said, "We just want to thank you for creating this place. We enjoy what you have done and have been back many times."

I asked them how many times, and they said, "We've been here sixteen times in the past five years, and we just love it."

We'd only been open eight years, and they'd already come to visit *sixteen times*. That told me our hard work had paid off. Creating something that people like is not about ego; it's about pride; it's about loving your customers; it's about working hard and coming up with a product that hits the mark and meets exactly what people are looking for.

This project was one of the biggest challenges in my life—it was in the middle of nowhere, developed without any loans, and there had been no prior successful properties in the area.

But where the first year or two in Cabo was the most stressful time in my life, in Loreto I felt very calm and confident. It was a lot of work, but it felt like an adventure. I started working in this industry when I was nineteen, and Loreto has felt like the crescendo of everything I've learned along the way.

Not bad for a guy from Rhode Island who left home with seven hundred bucks in his pocket!

CONCLUSION

My daughters all went to the American School in Puerto Vallarta, which encourages students to spend eleventh grade at a school in a different country, so they get more experience out of life than can be taught in a classroom. Brenda chose to go to a school in Toronto (very cold in the winter), and Rebecca went to Zug in Switzerland.

When her junior year approached, Jewel put some thought into it and decided to go to England for her study-abroad program. (I think the *Harry Potter* books had some appeal!) She applied, took the test, did online video interviews, and was accepted to three different elite schools.

Jewel chose to attend Brighton, a school that's about three hours outside of London by train. It's a big campus with both British and foreign students. She's in a dorm with sixteen other girls her age, and she's met so many people from different places—she has friends from Japan, Holland, Russia, and Ukraine. She loves it there.

It's like a light came on for her—she's passionate about everything now. She started a book club at her school and wants to write her first novel. She's going to school dances, and she was even in a play.

Her guidance counselor sent an email that said, "It's been a pleasure to be Jewel's tutor this year and watch her settle in. She's surpassed all of her requirements, which is reflected in her grades and her performance on exams. Her acting in the drama show was a particular highlight, and I was impressed with her poise and line delivery."

If there's anything I have ever done in my life that made all my work worth it, it was being able to send my daughters to these school experiences.

REPLACE YOURSELF AND MOVE UP

When I was in Waikiki, this Texan named Joe Caruso took over sales and marketing for the group in Hawaii. He would put on motivational seminars for us, and one of those talks he gave was about a concept that would stick with me for the rest of my life: replace yourself and move up.

I saw that as a challenge, because even in my limited work experience, most people—especially managers—really protected their jobs. They didn't want anyone learning or growing too much because they felt threatened. As time went by, I saw that they either didn't grow…or they ended up being replaced anyway. They prevented themselves from growing, out of fear, because they were waiting for someone else to pick them instead of creating their own growth.

Ever since then, I've made that my philosophy. It has been my mindset my entire career—a plan that was just as set in my management strategy as breathing is set in my life strategy. Replace yourself and move up. And it works.

When I became a manager, I did the opposite of the people I worked for. I made copies of all my materials and made the people in my training sessions take notes during meetings. We practiced role-playing and I taught them everything I could, so they could be successful at their jobs.

I always tried to hire the best people I could find to build the team. But maybe only one in twenty people you hire in sales are going to stay with you long term. So how do you keep good people working for you? If they don't see growth with you, they're going to quit and go somewhere else. A lot of companies have that problem of losing people because they don't see a job they can grow into.

But if you keep replacing yourself, there's always a growth opportunity for the people below you.

Make it an intentional decision for your career: replace yourself and move up. Don't let the fear stop you. Fear is the mortal enemy to humanity because it stops people from even trying. Overcome your fears. There might be setbacks; it might not be the golden road, but it will definitely be better than just staying in the same job you aren't passionate about for thirty years.

If you're going to replace yourself and move up, especially in a company setting, you have to know what the next level is. You have to know where you want to go before you can replace yourself and move up there—and there's always a new level to grow into.

That philosophy continues to work today.

A few months ago, we had a big company-wide conference, and we brought in motivational speakers for three days. As one of the owners, they asked me to come up and talk. I wasn't sure what to say at first, but what kept coming back to me was exactly what I'd heard all those years before, back in Hawaii: replace yourself and move up, because that's what I've done all my career—and that's what I'm going to keep doing.

I'm one of the most successful resort developers. But I'll never discover what's next for me out there if I don't replace myself and move up!

I recently had meetings with my top executives to say, "Hey, I'm ready to replace myself again."

I don't know yet exactly what moving up looks like for the next stage of my journey, but I'm interested in finding out.

THE TEST OF TIME

After ten years in business, we had a party at Felipe's, my restaurant in Puerto Vallarta, with dinner and champagne, to celebrate standing the test of time.

You don't have to sacrifice happiness to have longevity in your career. But if you don't take some time off, you're going to burn yourself out and get tunnel vision. Tunnel vision occurs when you do the same thing every day, and then you don't see the changes happening around you.

I was talking with one of my managers recently, and I told him, "You have to take your vacation time; it's mandatory."

He looked at me and said, "Gosh, I thought you would be making me work."

I make vacations mandatory in my company because I know that an important part of success is having balance.

> Several years ago, researchers out of Columbia University put a five-dollar bill on the sidewalk in front of a coffee shop, and then watched to see how many people stopped to pick it up. Only a very small percentage did. When the researchers interviewed the people who walked by, they said they hadn't noticed the money. They had tunnel vision.
>
> The study also showed that the people who *did* stop were more likely to be well educated, enlightened, and the boss of a company.

You also want to reward yourself along the way. I'm not talking about stupid stuff like going out partying until six in the morning (or buying a Rolex like Fernando and I did!). Take your family or significant other on a cruise or a nice vacation, something that's beneficial for all of you. Staying mentally healthy is vital, and if you can also have a great vacation, that's priceless.

I have taken three months off a year for the past ten years or so, which allows me to have a life outside of work.

If all you're doing all the time is just working, your life is contained in that work environment. In order to have a life outside of work, you have to create it by breaking free, having some fun, and celebrating all the good times you have on your journey of success.

WHAT'S NEXT?

People ask me if I ever plan to retire, and I tell them I don't know what that means. Even my partner asked, "When are you planning to retire?"

I told him, honestly, "What would I do?"

The Villa Group is still growing. We're opening up a brand-new resort in Cabo, Villa La Valencia, with very modern architecture, a unique design, and a pool network with a lazy river around the property. I still want to be involved with new properties; I just don't want to do it all the time.

But I don't ever see myself quitting 100 percent, because I think I have the best situation possible. I can go anywhere in the world and do anything, and I can still work. I have no stress and no need to retire.

In the beginning of my career, I wanted money and a new car. But I have those—and so much more—so what do I want to do now? What I'm looking at now is not so much about new projects; I'm looking more at the journey of life, what success and money actually mean.

It's amazing to consider how much learning what money is and how to provide a service that people like and want did for me.

I believe it was worth it to skip a few parties and sacrifice some of my youth to have this current success. I worked ten-hour days, seven days a week, when other people my age were going out drinking and partying. Sure, I went out, but I was diligent about work for decades. Even at the time, I told myself, "I'm going to do this now so that when I get older, I can take the time to do what I want."

I'm glad I committed to working when I was younger. I worked hard, and there were sacrifices I made along the way, but it was all worth it to have the freedom of life I have right now. The freedom to wake up in the morning and own my time, knowing that I don't have to stress about commitments or having to do things I don't want to do.

> I was just in New York to meet with my investment bankers, BNY Mellon, in their fiftieth floor penthouse office of the METLIFE building, looking out over the sweeping views of the city. There were fifteen of them and only one of me, to review my portfolio—what a great life experience. Still not bad for a guy who left home at the age of nineteen with only seven hundred dollars to his name!

The decisions we make accumulate over a lifetime. When you get older, I hope they add up to something positive for you, as has happened to me.

My oldest daughter, Brenda, just got her doctorate in psychology, has two kids, and is incredibly ambitious. She wants to join the business, so she's started attending meetings virtually.

My daughter Rebecca worked at the Mexican embassy in Washington, DC and is now taking graduate courses at George Washington University.

You read about my daughter Jewel at the beginning of this chapter, and my son, Owen, who wants to help me design a resort. He's still in high school, so we'll see what happens as he gets older, but I see no reason why he can't go to college and get experience with development if that's the path he wants to take.

I told them early on that the business would be part of their lives but they didn't have to be part of it if it wasn't their passion. I want them to be successful and happy, to find their place in the world, to grow up and be friends with everybody.

And as for me? I want to go on more journeys—journeys throughout the world, and journeys of more learning. I am more passionate about continuing my education about life and how the world works than I am about making another million dollars. When you quit learning, everything is the same, and you might as well roll over and die.

I'm having a new, 164-foot yacht built so I can escape for a while and wake up in the morning with a different view. I've owned a yacht since 2007, and the lifestyle is amazing. Now, I want to do some longer cruises—to South America, Colombia, Panama, Belize. West to New Zealand, Bora Bora, Tahiti, and Fiji.

I hope new things keep coming up, and that I am still discovering new things every day. I want to continue having the experience of a lifetime.

ANYTHING IS POSSIBLE

As you read my story and saw what I've achieved, you may have thought to yourself, *Those aren't the same things I want.*

That's fine! The things I've accomplished may not be the same for everyone, but what I have learned along the way can help anyone get what they want for themselves.

Look around at those who do have what you would like to have; people you would like to be like at their age; and come up with what feels right and personal to you. Learn what they did right, and formulate your own goals in life. Find what appeals to you and has meaning for your journey.

Be realistic as you come up with your plan, and recognize that you're not going to achieve your dreams overnight. Have perseverance to achieve your goals—through every iteration of your plan, from A to Z.

Then get rid of any baggage you may have been carrying around for too long, weighing you down. Who your parents were, where you came from—dump all that in a suitcase and put it in your closet where it doesn't affect you anymore.

Then you have to jump. Life is a leap of faith, and you have to go all-in.

If you can do all that, then I can't think of anything that can ever stop you from accomplishing everything you want to do.

ACKNOWLEDGMENTS

First, I'd like to acknowledge the most influential person in my life, my mom. She is always a positive person.

I'd also like to thank my kids. Besides my unconditional love for them, one time I was in an emotional business meeting and I yelled, "I HAVE KIDS TO SUPPORT!"

I also want to acknowledge the people at Scribe, especially Jenny :))) Thanks so much for your time and effort...

ABOUT THE AUTHOR

OWEN PERRY, a founding Partner in The Villa Group, is a hotelier and developer.

With thirty-eight years of development experience in Mexico, The Villa Group's impressive portfolio of twelve resort properties, includes hotels, residential full-ownership residences, and mixed-use properties. Known for its quality design and construction along with the sales and management of Five Star resorts, spas, and restaurants, the company was also a founder of Resort Communications (now ResortCom International, LLC), based in Las Vegas, since 1985.

Mr. Perry's latest endeavor is a 1,600-acre mixed-use development in Loreto, Mexico, which includes The Villa Group's Villa del Palmar Loreto with a championship golf course, seven condo-hotel lots, 140 home lots, and commercial space. He also owns a variety of restaurants in Cabo San Lucas.

Owen founded REmexico Real Estate to bring a new level of

professionalism to real estate transactions in Mexico, serving clients with a strong understanding of property law, a commitment to due diligence, and clear title, and premium support to foreign buyers and sellers.

DanzanteBay.com